THE

LQ

SOLUTION

INFLUENCE, IMPACT, AND INCREASE

P.20
You are a World Chaser!

DR. KEITH JOHNSON

The LQ SOLUTION
Influence, Impact, and Increase

Unless otherwise noted, all Scripture quotations are from THE HOLY BIBLE, NEW INTERNATIONAL VERSION®, Copyright © 1973, 1978, 1984 by Biblica, Inc. Used by permission of Zondervan. All rights reserved.

Scripture quotations marked NKJV are from The New King James Version. Copyright © 1982 by Thomas Nelson, Inc. Used by permission. All rights reserved. Scriptures marked KJV are from the King James Version.

Scriptures marked NLT are taken from the Holy Bible, New Living Translation, copyright © 1996, 2004, 2007 by Tyndale House Publishers, Inc., Carol Stream, Illinois 60189. All rights reserved.

Scriptures marked MSG are taken from The Message Remix 2.0: The Bible in Contemporary Language Navpress; Kindle Edition.

Published by KJI Publishing

P.O. Box 6777 Spring Hill, FL 34611 | 352-597-8775

Published by Camden House Books, LLC

Post Office Box 727 | Broken Arrow, OK 74011

www.KeithJohnson.TV
KJ@KeithJohnson.TV

ISBN: 978-0-9855167-0-3

Printed in Canada
1 2 3 4 5 6 / 15 14 13 12

What Others Are Saying About the LQ Solution

"Keith Johnson has held the title of America's #1 Confidence Coach for many years—and for a good reason. He not only educates, he also motivates and imparts a "special something" from heaven into the lives of his listeners and students by encouraging the release of their hidden potential.

"I'm particularly excited about *The LQ Solution* because it unfolds the real roadmap to influence, impact, and increase in both the leader and the student. I offered a private (yet thunderous) applause for Dr. Johnson as I read Chapter Seven about making a 'Not To Do List.' Those of us who have served in leadership wish we had read this chapter many years ago.

"Get ready for a quantum leap into a higher level of leadership as you read *The LQ Solution*."

–Dr. Dave Williams
Bishop of Mount Hope Church Global Network

"I like books that tell stories succinctly and provide pragmatic ways to apply important principles—Dr. Keith Johnson's books do that. In his latest book, *The LQ Solution: Influence, Impact, and Income*, Dr. Johnson draws on time-tested life experiences of himself and other leaders and gives solutions that produce results."

–Dr. Samuel R. Chand
Author of Cracking Your Church's Culture Code

"YOU can make a significant difference on this earth. *The LQ Solution* can help. *The LQ Solution* is page after page of practical wisdom YOU can use 24/7/365 to maximize YOUR potential and equip YOUR team to make the difference YOU want to make!"

–Bobb Biehl
Executive Mentor Since 1976

"*The LQ Solution* provides powerful principles for the leader desiring to achieve a life of success and balance. Keith Johnson does a masterful job of weaving his powerful insights, illustrations, and 'post-it' applications of God's timeless truth providing the reader with real leadership solutions."

–Dennis Worden
Former Vice President of Injoy Life Club with John Maxwell

"I recently finished editing a book project with Dr. Keith Johnson titled, *The LQ Solution*. It's the best leadership book for church leaders I have read and edited since I wrote the study guides for John Maxwell's *21 Irrefutable Laws of Leadership* and *Fail Forward*. I recommend you read the book today and then seriously consider having Keith come for leadership training and ministering to your congregation."

–Dr. Larry Keefauver
Bestselling Author and International Teacher

"Keith Johnson's new book, *The LQ Solution*, is on the leading edge of helping every believer maximize their leadership potential. This book is filled with many golden nuggets. Opening this book is like opening a treasure chest! Get ready to get rich—rich with the wisdom, knowledge, and skills you need to become a success in any of life's endeavors."

–John P. Kelly
President of LEAD

DEDICATION

I dedicate this book to my "BIG FIVE" leadership mentors who have taught me almost everything I know:

John C. Maxwell

John P. Kelly

Bobb Biehl

Samuel Chand

Dwight Shirley

ACKNOWLEDGMENTS

I acknowledge and appreciate the following people for help with getting this manuscript ready for publication:

Larry Keefauver

Dave Hail

John P. Kelly

Wendy K. Walters

Angela Rickabaugh Shears

Kathy Curtis

CONTENTS

Section II: What Is a Leader?

Final Word

Resources

"The church is painfully in need of leaders," lamented the English Methodist preacher William Sangster. "I wait to hear a voice and no voice comes. I would rather listen than speak—but there is no clarion voice to listen to."

"If the world is to hear the church's voice today, leaders are needed who are authoritative, spiritual, and sacrificial. Authoritative, because people desire reliable leaders who know where they are going and are confident of getting there. Spiritual, because without a strong relationship to God, even the most attractive and competent person cannot lead people to God. Sacrificial, because this trait follows the model of Jesus, who gave Himself for the whole world and who calls us to follow in His steps."

—J. Oswald Chambers
Spiritual Leadership: A Commitment to
Excellence for Every Believer

CHAPTER ONE

MAXIMIZE YOUR INFLUENCE, IMPACT, AND INCOME

Is it possible to love God with all your heart but not make a difference in the lives of others?

Lula Jones was an eighty-two-year-old member of the first church I pastored. She was one of the hippest seniors I had ever met. She drove a fire engine red car with a license plate on the front: *Foxy Grandma.* She was also very active in our church and deeply spiritual. As a matter of fact, she would arrive at service early to pray and read her Bible. In spite of my youth and foolish mistakes, she loved and supported me. I loved Lula.

It happened suddenly; Lula was diagnosed with cancer and died soon thereafter. The day of her funeral, only five people were in attendance. I was embarrassed and upset because none of our church members showed up. Only three cars were in the funeral procession to her graveside service. Did her life really make an impact on others?

While driving to Lula's burial site I thought, *When I die, I don't want only three cars to take me to my burial site. I want to make such a difference in people's lives that the whole city will have to shut down.* Then this question came to me, *Is it possible for people to love God with all their hearts yet not impact and influence others?* Sadly, the answer is, "Yes, it is possible, and in fact, probable." Lula and several thousand other highly spiritual people are proof that happens every day.

This led me to think about the following questions:

- Why do some people have tremendous impact, influence, and income, and others produce very little?

- How can we predict who will do something big and beautiful for God and those who will make little difference?

- Why do some people acquire extraordinary wealth and influence, while others don't?

When staring at death, I asked, "Why did I waste so much energy on things that didn't matter?" —Ric Elias

Your life perspective changes based on your points of view— past, current, or future (death). Are you looking at your life from where you started, where you are now, or from the end—at the very last moments of your life? Most people view their lives from the past or present. But when you review your life from the end, everything takes on a new meaning. From the beginning and now, we tend to focus on our survival and successes—from the end, we are forced to focus on impact and making a difference. From the future or the end you start asking yourself more challenging questions such as:

- Did I use my life, energy, and resources to make a difference?

- Did I leave the world in better shape than the way I found it?

- Did I live for a cause larger than myself?

- Did I waste my life doing things that did not matter for eternity?

Throughout this book we will be examining your perspective on life, your career, your ministry, and your relationship with God, yourself, and others. Also throughout this book are LQ Solutions meant as post-it mind notes—crucial keys to keep life moving forward, expand your boundaries, and make the biggest, most powerful and positive impact possible.

LQ Solution: Connecting to the fact that you will die one day is a powerful tool to shift your thinking from influence to impact and awaken your inner leader.

What about You?

Here is what I discern about you—you want to make a significant difference in your life and the lives of others! You want to know your life matters. However, you haven't yet reaped the results you really want. You need direction. You need a clear sense of what to do next. You also need real solutions to the current problems you are facing. And you want to live life at your maximum potential!

LQ Solution: God's gift to you is your potential. Your gift to God is what you do with it.

Potential is not who you are now, but who you can become. Potential is not what you are doing now, but what you can do in the future. Potential is not what you have at this moment, but what you can own in the future. Potential is not who you are helping at this moment, but the multitudes you could be helping in the future. Potential is crying out from your future saying, "You can be, do, have, and help more. Keep reaching!"

IQ, EQ, or GQ?

Social scientists in the study of human potential have created tests to evaluate a person's level of achievement in life. These tests are supposed predictors of a person's future educational achievements, potential, quality of relationships, job performance, and income. In 1905, French psychologist Alfred Binet developed the first IQ (Intelligence Quotient) test. The thesis was that a high score on this test measured a person's intelligence.

One researcher in IQ made an interesting observation:

> *Having a high IQ can become a disincentive to action. People with high IQs and analytical abilities often can see more and more layers to a problem, and as a result, they become paralyzed because they can't see their way through to a solution. When action is needed, they may be unable to take it. Psychologists have studied relationships between IQ and leadership. They have found that during times of relative calm, when there is no great premium on quick action, people with higher IQs are more effective as leaders than are those with lower IQs. But in times of stress, the relationship actually reverses itself. High IQ becomes an impediment to action, and the higher-IQ individual becomes a less effective leader than the lower-IQ one. Thus, the ability to think through alternative courses of action is important, but it is equally important to know when to wait and when to act.*[1]

So, according to this researcher, IQ plays a role in leadership, but there's more. For example, our Emotional Quotient (EQ) also impacts how a person leads. Daniel Goleman's book, *Emotional Intelligence*, showed the world that success and achievement were determined not only by IQ, but also by EQ. Emotional Intelligence is the measurement of a person's ability to manage one's own emotional state, the emotional state of others, and the emotional state of a group of people. We even have fashion experts for men who have successfully produced the *GQ* magazine that evaluates and educates men on fashion trends.

What Is Missing?

Do you know really bright, emotionally strong, and beautifully dressed people who never seem to achieve anything and are always broke? On the other side, do you know people who are not very bright, emotionally healthy, and poorly dressed who have achieved incredible things in life?

In my sixteen years of studying human potential, I have found that influence, impact, and increase depend on something beyond our IQ, EQ, or GQ. I have discovered that a person's LQ— Leadership Quotient—is a significant and primary predictor of the size of a person's *impact, influence, and income.*

What is LQ? LQ is the study of your personal leadership quotient, which brings men and women to the maximum of their God-given potential!

Leadership Quotient Definition

Leadership Quotient (LQ) is a composite measure of a person's leadership skills that positively influences people to join that person in achieving desired outcomes that benefit others.

Research has shown that maximizing human potential is a primary factor influencing the health, wealth, and growth of every person, business, church, nonprofit organization, and nation.

Therefore, every organization benefits greatly when the LQ of each person in the organization is increased.

LQ Potential Is Within Each Person!
(Even if you don't think so.)

Every human being on the planet has the potential to become a leader; most people do not have the confidence and courage, however, to cultivate their LQ. I've heard people described as "born leaders." But I must disagree. There are too many examples in history of ordinary people who developed into great leaders by the force of the need at hand—and everyone has that ability.

You would be surprised what you could do if there was simply a demand placed on your inner leadership potential. It's quite possible, a 90 percent chance in my own personal findings, you don't want to be a leader or you have not considered yourself a leader of any kind. Whether or not you have viewed yourself as a leader, you will be surprised to learn just how many ways you are already a leader, especially to those close to you.

LQ Solution: Sociologists tell us that even the most introverted individual will influence ten thousand other people during his or her lifetime.[2]

You will also be surprised by the fact that many people whom you consider to be powerful and influential leaders never wanted to be leaders, and even to this day do not see themselves as leaders. I know. I have coached and consulted privately with many of these people, some of whom you will read about later in this book.

Leadership in its basic form is simply your ability to influence and inspire people in a positive way. Do you influence people around you in a positive way? Do you inspire and encourage people? If so, you have already been using your Leadership Quotient.

You do not have to be the president of a billion dollar corporation, the president of a country, or the pastor of a megachurch to be a leader. Start with your family, friends, church, school, or workplace. You can become a successful, trusted leader right where you are at the moment. Learning how to expose, develop, and then use your LQ is an exciting life process, and I am excited to help you begin the journey!

Now Is the Time

Just as each person possesses intelligence (IQ), emotions (EQ), and the ability to dress fashionably (GQ), so each person has Leadership Quotient (LQ) within. This potential can and must be developed. Just as intelligence and emotional health can be increased, deepened, and matured, so can your LQ. If your LQ is stunted or underdeveloped, you may need a personal awakening of your inner leader.

One of the reasons why there is a demand for leaders is that too many people, regrettably, would rather be led than assume leadership responsibility. When you are ready to accept the challenges of leadership, you will find many wonderful opportunities waiting to help you break away from the pack and to build on your achievements for future success.

If you are struggling with financial challenges, bored at your current job, discouraged about your life achievements, unsure about how to grow your organization, frustrated with people who lack motivation, or just simply tired of not seeing real change in your life, then you need to start thinking, feeling, and acting differently. Through the principles and truths set forth in this book, you will learn how to implement solutions to overcome your current life and leadership problems.

When the country is in chaos, everybody has a plan to fix it—but it takes a leader of real understanding to straighten things out (Proverbs 28:2 MSG).

The problems you are facing as an individual can be corrected as you first learn to lead yourself. Everyone has problems, but they become real problems if you are facing the same ones you were facing last year. As Dr. Phil would say, "How has that been working for you?" Remember, *leadership is always the problem, and leadership is always the SOLUTION.*

Men make history and not the other way around. In periods where there is no leadership, society stands still. Progress occurs when courageous, skillful leaders seize the opportunity to change things for the better. —President Harry S. Truman

Maximizing Your Impact, Influence, and Income Starts Right Now!

I regularly meet people who are surprised to learn that their own LQ level is an important part of increasing their impact, influence, and income. It's true. Whatever we do in life, our personal achievements depend on our growth as leaders. All institutions need leaders. We know this is true whether that institution is a church, nation, business, school, factory, or family.

The world prizes and rewards people who have the guts to unleash their potential and manifest their inner leader. Influence, riches, and power have been claimed by those who, by virtue of their desire for a better future, are able to attract the loyalty, respect, and service of others. People with high LQs in all walks of life are in constant demand. And guess what the by-product of higher demand produces? Higher perceived value and more money.

Just imagine for a moment if you, like the biblical Joseph, knew by divine revelation that in the future you would be the leader of a nation, president of the company you work for, or the senior pastor of a large church. What would you have to know, do, or become to be ready to accept that opportunity? God has an amazing plan for your future. He is preparing you for something that you do not know is coming.

Please know that your growth inwardly and externally as a leader starts today. The time to prepare for your future opportunity is not when opportunity taps you on the shoulder. The time to prepare is now!

LQ Solution: The more a person knows God, the more he will know himself—and LQ begins to emerge.

When humankind became disconnected from God, the results were horrific. We became blinded to the understanding of:

- Who we really are - Identity
- Why are we here - Purpose
- Where we came from - Heritage
- Where we are going - Destiny
- What we are capable of achieving - Potential

LQ is about self-discovery. It is about your commitment to becoming the real you. Human beings were the only creatures created in the image and likeness of God. This means that you have God's DNA, His very nature. An important dynamic of that aspect is God's ability to create, imagine, plan, set priorities, and make decisions. In other words, inside you is God's LQ that needs to be awakened, discovered, and developed.

Leadership Is in Every Believer's DNA

This book is your challenge to become the leader inherent in your DNA and your destiny as a child of God. As a believer, every Christian is a new creation in Christ Jesus (see 2 Corinthians 5:17). The DNA of Jesus has been implanted in each believer—His nature for serving, leading, discipling, coaching, and teaching is part of our new nature in Christ. Apostle Paul admonishes others to follow his example as he followed Christ (see 1 Corinthians 11:1).

At a very minimum, we are leaders by example when we begin to follow Christ. Growing and maturing as Christian examples, leaders, and disciplers must be a priority in our lives because leadership is implanted into our new nature.

The Joel Osteen Factor

Today, Joel Osteen is a leader whose impact, influence, and income are obvious. Whether or not you like his style, smile, or theology, he has a list of amazing achievements: pastors the largest church in America; is a *New York Times* bestselling author and popular television guest; and speaks to sold-out crowds at major stadiums worldwide.

However, Joel constantly talks about how he never imagined, while working in the media department for his father, that he had the ability to be a public speaker. As a matter of fact, in his first sermon after his dad died he said, "It's a miracle I am even up at this pulpit." John Osteen, his father, saw Joel's potential, but Joel did not see it in himself until there was a demand placed on his inner LQ.

LQ Solution: God sees more in you than you see in yourself.

Most modern leadership books start out with the proverbial cry, "Where are the leaders?" or "Who will be the next breed of leaders?" These are valid and important questions, but my questions are: "What if the spiritual leaders needed for this season are already in our churches? What if it is you? And you, like Joel, are not even aware of it?"

I often wonder how many other Joel Osteens are currently working behind the scenes. I wonder how many leaders we have who blindly go to church every Sunday, but have not been awakened to their Leadership Quotient and real potential to become the leader they have been created to be.

LQ Solution: God is a master at taking ordinary people and using them to do extraordinary things.

I also wonder how many leaders have, for whatever reason, lost their impact, influence, and maybe even their income. For every one spiritual giant falling publically, there are scores who are falling quietly behind the closed doors of the church. Without the paparazzi, media explanation, or fanfare, their followers silently slip away because they no longer trust their leaders.

Perhaps the greatest need of this season is not looking for new leaders but in:

- Awakening ordinary people to their extraordinary potential for greatness, and

- Maximizing the leaders who already exist.

An Ordinary Person

Does a person working the cash register at McDonald's or Sam's Club have the potential to become a future leader?

Kevin Turner is a great example of how an ordinary person can achieve extraordinary results by developing their LQ. Kevin started working at the cash register at Sam's Club. However, he became a serious student of the subject of leadership. He worked his way up the company and eventually became the CEO of Sam's Club. Then he landed another opportunity as the COO of another "small company" called Microsoft. He currently influences more than 65,000 employees and over $65 billion in revenues.

The apostle Paul writes, "For we are God's masterpiece. He has created us anew in Christ Jesus, so we can do the good things he planned for us long ago" (Ephesians 2:10 NLT). You are a masterpiece created in Christ to accomplish good and great things. That's potential! That's Leadership Quotient!

If you do not discover and develop your LQ, you will not be able to fulfill your life assignment. The result is devastating! God's purpose for putting you here on this planet is for you to solve some sort of difficult problem or meet a specific need for your generation. If you don't grow your inner leader, you could deprive the next generation of a problem's solution or not meeting a desperate need. God has placed you here for such a time as this! The timing of your birth was precise and prophetic.

This book will help you develop your Leadership Quotient, your "masterpiece" potential, and your calling in Christ. This is your year to grow your LQ so you can maximize your impact, influence, and income as a Christian leader!

The LQ within you is waiting to be discovered and developed. *Before reading further*, please turn to Appendix A at the end of this book titled The LQ Solution Profile. Complete the assessment and keep a record of your score. Then when you complete reading this book and implementing the steps at the end of each chapter for unleashing your LQ, retake the profile and celebrate the improvement in your score as well as how you are beginning to maximize your influence, impact, and income.

Unleash Your LQ

To help unleash your LQ, I've placed some important, thought-provoking questions at the end of each chapter. Consider your answers carefully.

- How long after I die do I want my life to make a difference?

- What can I do to make the most significance for God?

- How would I like to be remembered?

- What have I always dreamed of contributing to the world?

- If I could accomplish only three measurable things before I die, what would those things be?

Endnotes

1. Bill Service and Dave Arnott, *The Leadership Quotient* (New York: iUniverse Inc, 1996), 106.

2. John Maxwell, *Developing the Leader Within You* (Nashville: Thomas Nelson Publishers, 2005), 3.

Your

REPORT CARD

In Section I, six "As" for Leadership Intelligence
will be detailed and discussed:

Awareness

Advancement

Alignment

Axiom

Assurance

Achievement

Each A on your report card brings you closer to maximizing the
influence, impact, and income of your life, church or ministry, or
organization.

Are You Aware of Your Potential?

As we discuss the awesome task of tapping our true and full potential, it is essential that we come to appreciate how important each one of us is and how special we are to God. If you were aware of how much power and worth you have, the first thing that would be affected is your attitude toward yourself.

–Myles Munroe, *Understanding Your Potential*

The number one issue I see with leaders is that they don't know who they are.

–Bobb Biehl, *Executive Mentor*

CHAPTER TWO

AWARENESS

There Is a Leader in You!

How important is it to you that you become everything God has called you to be? I ask this question of my audiences around the world. Warning! Be careful how quickly you answer this question.

A knee-jerk reaction is, "It is very important. I want to become everything that God wants me to become." When I ask people that question they enthusiastically say, "YES!" However, when I ask them to clearly define what it is that God wants them to become, most people have no clue what it is.

Can you clearly articulate what God wants you to become? If you don't know who you are supposed to become, how can you ever aim at becoming that person?

Let me ask you another coaching question, "When you think of a leader, who are the five people who instantly come to mind?" List below.

1. _____

2. _____

3. _____

4. _____

5. _____

In the past if you asked me this question, I would instantly see pictures in my mind of people like Abraham Lincoln, Dr. Martin Luther King Jr., Winston Churchill, Jesus Christ, Gandhi, or maybe the current president of the United States. Hardly anybody would argue about this list of leaders. Right?

There is one major and I mean *major* problem with this list. This problem caused me to live a broke, busted, and disgusted life for years! And it may be causing you to live below your very best. What is the problem? I didn't write my name on the list of people I think about when I think of a leader. I bet you are a lot like I used to be. You don't really see yourself as a leader. Or maybe you really don't want to be a leader. Maybe the very mention of the word leader causes you to shut down emotionally. I know how you feel. Stay with me for a few chapters as we take this journey together to discover how we can make a greater difference—as leaders.

The Three-Step Discovery Formula: A→C→R

Your journey to becoming everything you were supposed to be starts with Awareness (A). When you have greater awareness of your thoughts, how you really see yourself, you can make the right Choice (C) to become the right person you were designed to be. When you make the right choices in life, you begin to experience better Results (R). With a better awareness of what God wants you to become, you will say, "Okay! If that is what God wants me to become, I will accept that and begin my journey to personal transformation."

I mentioned Joel Osteen's trek to awareness of his Leadership Quotient earlier. Initially, he was not fully aware of his leadership potential as he sat in an editing room working on his father's messages. But awareness came to him. You, too, need to be awakened to your true Leadership Quotient in Christ. The insights in this book will do more than just help you "learn" that you are a leader. Learning comes from educating the mind. I want your inner self to be "awakened" by revelation so you will *know* without a shadow of a doubt that you *are* a leader. Learning is all about the mind. Knowing is all about the heart.

**LQ Solution: There is a leader inside you
screaming to get out.**

An Eagle or a Turkey?

Most of us are not leaders because, in our hearts, we don't believe that is who we are. The moment you discover who you really are, the need for others to title you, label you, or pigeonhole you becomes unnecessary. You are an eagle not a turkey. Throughout this book, we are going to open the cage so the inner leader inside you will emerge. That leader is like a newly born eaglet—it is already an eagle, just like you are already a leader. However, the eaglet needs to be nurtured, developed, and trained to become the bold and beautiful adult eagle it is suppose to be.

**LQ Solution: You must see the leader in you. What is
seeable becomes believable.
What is believable becomes possible.**

Your mind is your most valuable asset. Your mind needs a hero (a picture of what you can become) and a goal (a picture of what you would like to achieve). Your mind is designed in such a way that it needs pictures fed into it of who you want to become, what you want to do, what you want to have, and who you want to help. You are motivated to become the picture of how you see yourself. Once you feed your mind those images, your mind goes to work on discovering how to make those pictures become a reality in your life. But *if you have no real picture in your mind, you live life by default instead of living life by design.*

I must admit, I am an optimist; and by nature I am a positive thinker and a big dreamer. However, on March 16, 2002, I was totally unhappy with the results I was getting in my personal and professional life. I was broke, up to my eyeballs in debt, and had to move into my mother-in-law's ten-foot by ten-foot bedroom. For my own personal impact, influence, and income to increase, I had to come to a place of awareness that I was a leader. Then I made a choice to improve the picture of how I saw myself. My personal achievements, happiness, and income started to change for the better.

Today, I travel the world, live in the house of my dreams, and I am debt free. I spend my life influencing successful people who have influence over others. I have coached senior pastors from small, medium, to megasize churches, celebrities, denominational presidents, successful business leaders, government leaders, millionaires, and even a billionaire.

My biblically-based success and leadership principles have now influenced both the church and secular markets. My previous book, *The Confidence Solution—Reinvent Yourself, Explode Your Business, Skyrocket Your Income,* was published by Penguin books and became an instant best seller by reaching #21 in Amazon's motivation and business category. I am a frequent television guest, appearing on popular shows and stations such as New York's PIX 11, *Fox Business News, The Tom Sullivan Show*, CBS, ABC, TBN, Daystar, and many others. I have been recognized by *Women's World* magazine as one of America's "Ultimate Experts," which is the most-read women's magazine in the world.

I did this all because I realized the importance of LQ. I purposely discovered and developed it—and I'm so glad I did. What I am sharing with you throughout these pages will bring you similar results of success and fulfillment.

God's DNA Spells L...E...A...D...E...R

The Bible is the original book on leadership. The author, God, is the first leader we meet in the Bible (see Genesis 1:1). What was He doing in the beginning? What all leaders do—*creating.* The first revelation God gave of Himself is that of Creator. Why? The first revelation He wants you to get is that of a creator not a victim. You were created to be creative.

The Bible gives you pictures of what a leader looks, talks, and acts like. In the Bible are stories about Adam, Eve, Abraham, Moses, David, Deborah, Nehemiah, Joseph, Esther, Ruth, Jesus, the disciples, Paul, and others in leadership. As you read the Bible, you can easily build a library of LQ pictures in your mind.

As you study these LQ pictures, you will soon discover another image beginning to take shape. You will recognize this picture is you. You begin to see yourself, not as what you have been in your past, but the possibilities of what you are going to become in your future. This mental photograph should become your desired outcome. Your enemies will try to paint a picture in your mind of who you are at your worst. The picture you develop of yourself is crucial to determining your level of impact, influence, and income.

LQ Solution: It is not who you think you *are* that holds you back; it is who you think you are *not* that holds you back.

Since 1998, I have personally coached and consulted hundreds of senior pastors. When I start talking to them about increasing their LQ, I have heard this over and over, "I am not a leader. I am *just* a pastor." With one pastor of a thousand people, I spent an entire day helping him see he was a great leader. Once his inner leader was awakened to this fact, his confidence increased and his ministry exploded. Over the next two years, his ministry totally changed. He went from pastoring one church to starting and pastoring over twenty-three different successful churches.

Another pastor never saw himself as a leader. When I first meet him, I thought he probably led a church of several thousand people. His GQ was high; he knew how to dress like a successful leader on the outside. However, his LQ was in the toilet. He actually had only ten people in his church and had a one-man painting business. Now that he has been awakened to his leadership quotient, his church has grown tremendously and his one-man show painting business now has five crews painting in several counties.

One brilliant, young black man from the inner city of Chicago I have worked with over the years never saw himself as a leader of any kind. Yet, he has a very strategic and analytical mind. As a government employee, he knew the solutions to the problems his bosses were facing, but in meetings, he always kept his mouth shut in fear of being criticized. Once I helped him awaken his inner leader, he started to share his views and totally blew his superiors away. He was quickly promoted and eventually became part of history as he was elected to work on the transition team for President Obama.

Here is what I know I have in common with you—deep down inside, you really want to make a difference! You know that you have way more potential inside of you than you are manifesting at this very moment. You want to know that your life counted. That is why you bought this book. Right!

In a gentle way, you can shake the world.

—Mahatma Gandhi

After I speak at events, I usually go to my product table to meet and greet people. Many people thank me for inspiring them. Then I look the person right in the eyes and say, "Now go do something big and beautiful for God!" As I gaze into their eyes, I can tell that saying those words for some people is like pouring gasoline onto an already burning fire. However, many others graciously bow their heads and sheepishly walk away.

One of the most paralyzing belief systems most underachievers have is believing: "My life will not make a difference." This is the belief system of a professional victim and a person stuck in learned hopelessness. If you have believed the lie that you are too "small" to make a difference, then you have never been in a room with a small mosquito! Like Mahatma Gandhi said, "In a gentle way, you can shake the world."

Winston Churchill said, "The price of greatness is responsibility." Leaders take responsibility for their outcomes in life. Fear is rooted in the belief that you have no option or choice. Being a victim is a belief that others choose for you, thus allowing you the opportunity to blame others or events in your past.

On What Ship Do You Find Yourself?

Do you see yourself on the "Leader-*ship*" or the "Victim-*ship*"? In crisis times, the ship you are on determines whether you sink or stay afloat to your destination. The Victim ship always sinks and ends up at the bottom of the ocean. You can shift from Victim-ship to Leader-ship! Victims see all their limitations. Leaders see great opportunities and possibilities. Hopeless victims see only the problems. Confident leaders see the solutions. Victims make excuses. Leaders get results.

Consider these truisms:

- Victims *say*, "I've tried everything."
  Leaders *decide*, "There has got to be another way."

- Victims *wait* for their ship to come in.
  Leaders *jump* into the water and swim to the ship.

- Victims *cry*, "Why me?"
  Leaders *shout*, "It's up to me!"

- Victims say, "*I am frightened* of all the changes in the world!"
  Leaders say, "*I am inspired* by all changes in the world!"

- Victims are into **entertainment**.
  Leaders are into **education**.

To unleash and display to the world your inner leader, you must keep a proper mental perspective of life. *You are God's Kingdom heir, not life's victim!* It is time to climb the mountain to the very top of becoming everything you were called to be.

You never conquer a mountain. Mountains can't be conquered; you conquer yourself—your hopes, your fears.
–Jim Whitaker, first American to reach
the summit of Mount Everest

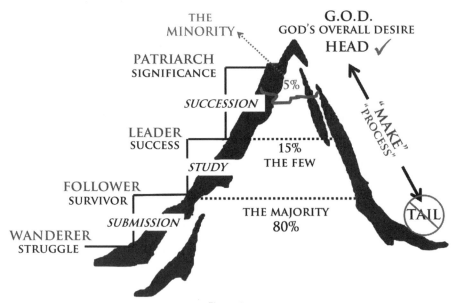

Figure 1
Leadership Advancement Mountain

So what does God really want us all to become? The leadership advancement mountain can paint a picture of the upward journey to maximizing your leadership potential. Deuteronomy 28:13 is the foundational scripture for the premise of this illustration:

And the Lord will make you the head and not the tail; you shall be above only, and not be beneath, if you heed the commandments of the Lord your God, which I command you today, and are careful to observe them.

The difference between where we are and where God wants to bring us is called *process*. As I mentioned in Chapter One, there are no "born leaders." Becoming a leader is a process. God wants to make us into the leaders He designed. Many Christians enjoy exciting worship services, miracles, signs and wonders, but many are not too excited about embracing the process of becoming the person they were destined to be. Jesus' call for the disciples to follow Him was not an invitation to a one-time event but a challenge to enter into a lifetime process of becoming persons of influence.

We all gravitate naturally to a life of ease. In church or ministry life, that means presenting events, seminars, etc. Attending hyped-up church services or another seminar may bring encouragement and raise expectations; however, allowing God to transform us into His new creation can be difficult, time-consuming, trying, and even painful.

Ministers and church members often find themselves addicted to events—avoiding the process of transformation. We choose momentary relief over personal improvement, easy over difficult, and instantaneous over process. However, God wants us to understand His Word as saying, "I am going to make you into something special." What, is the big question. The answer: "I am going to make you the head and not the tail. I am going to make you above and not beneath."

As we begin to discover that God's Overall Desire (G.O.D.) for us is to become like Christ the Leader, we realize that to be on the top means climbing, pushing, working, letting go of wrong thinking and excess baggage, and reaching beyond who we are to who we must become. So think about this: *If you are on top, doesn't that mean you are in a place where other people are looking up at you? Doesn't that mean you are in a place where other people are following you? If people are following you...that makes you a leader.*

LQ Solution: The more you sweat in training, the less you bleed in battle. –Motto of U.S. Navy Seals

Hard-core military personnel like the Navy Seals or Marines don't just happen; they are trained and developed during a process, beginning with boot camp. God's boot camp of leadership takes us from the bottom, as wanderers, to the top, as patriarch servant leaders whose lives bring others to Christ; we better the lives of other leaders, and then reproduce servant leaders.

Becoming a Leader Is a Process— Starting Is Essential

People can have great leadership potential, but it must be developed. We have to identify where we are on the Leadership Mountain (see Figure 1) so we know what season of life we are in, and then we can embrace personal transformation, make the right decisions, and grow to our full potential.

LQ Solution: Cut and polish your leadership potential with knowledge, skills, and service, and you will be in great demand throughout your life.

Looking at Figure 1, you will notice that becoming everything you are supposed to be happens in stages. Notice these stages:

Wanderer (struggle) (submit); Follower (survival) (study); Leader (success) (successor); Patriarch (significance) (legacy). However, we all start the process at the bottom of the mountain as Wanderers.

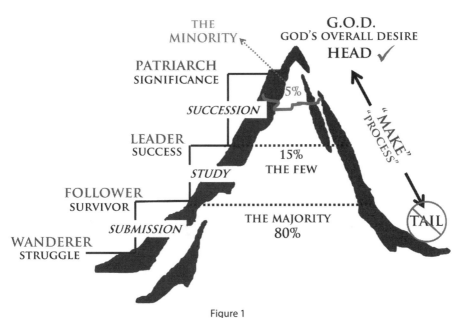

Figure 1
Leadership Advancement Mountain

STAGE 1 – WANDERER

- *Description of your current circumstances: Struggle*

- *Your heart's cry: "I need direction!"*

- *Internal Questions: "Why am I here? Where am I going?"*

- *Focus: Self-Centered*

- *Action word to exiting this season: Submit or surrender*

We all started out as wanderers and sojourners, didn't we? We were without God; we were without Christ and didn't know where we were going in life. We weren't on a journey, but rather a treadmill continually running fast but going nowhere. Wandering through life, we had no real sense of purpose or destiny. Like Kenny Rogers sang, "We were looking for love in all the wrong places." We lived life in a place of constant struggle, stress, and confusion. Remember those days?

If you are currently in this wandering stage, your first decision is to submit and surrender your life to Jesus Christ. Receive His love, acceptance, and forgiveness—and be free from the negative power of guilt and shame. If you have already done that, you are well on your way to being a Christ follower, and a leader of others.

STAGE 2 - FROM WANDERER TO FOLLOWER

- *Description of your current circumstances: Survival*

- *Your heart's cry: "I am tired of just barely getting by. I want to be a success."*

- *Internal Questions: "Will I ever make it? Will I make it as a leader? Will our organization make it next year? Will we be able to keep the doors open?"*

- *Focus: Self-Centered*

- *Action word to exiting this season: Study*

Hopefully you have already transitioned from a wanderer to a follower. When we submit ourselves to Christ, we become followers of Christ.

"Come, follow me," Jesus said, "and I will make you fishers of men" (Matthew 4:19).

However, the majority of the world and even Christians continue to struggle through life as followers of people, fads, and traditions rather than Him. Christ spoke to us about following Him to fulfill our destinies. We thought if we followed Him that every difficulty would disappear and life would be easy. But Christian living has no "easy button." To follow Him involves surrendering what *you* want for what *He* wants.

Bill Hybels describes the process of following Christ as *descending into greatness*. If you want to become a leader, you must start as a servant embracing surrender, humility, and transformation. Learning to follow is part of the process. Why? Because great followers become great leaders.

As long as you are a follower in anything, all you experience is survival. Why? Because you are only halfway up or still at the bottom of the mountain. Survival isn't leadership because all the money, influence, and power are on the top of the mountain, not halfway down or at the bottom.

LQ Solution: God wants you to be on top.

God desires to move followers from being high maintenance, low impact, low influence, and low income to low maintenance, high impact, high influence, and higher income. God never intended the church to operate in a survival mentality. We must move beyond a maintenance mentality to a leaders of transformation mentality.

Surviving isn't satisfactory. If you are just surviving and you know God has more for you, you have to transition out of the following mode into the leadership mode. The way to do that is to study and prepare yourself to become a leader. As you begin to grow in servanthood, excellence, knowledge, and understanding, you will start to achieve success, earn more money, and begin to see more power and influence in your life.

How do you transition out of follow-ship into leadership? By studying the subject of leadership—this way you become the best at what you do. Leaders are readers. (Consider earning your

Master's of Christian Leadership degree at Destiny College. See Appendix D.)

When you move from being a *good* follower to a *great* follower, you become a model or an example for others to follow. Good followers "dabble" at what they do. Great followers become "masters" at what they do. This is your first step toward a leadership lifestyle. As others watch you and are impacted by your example, excellence, coaching, discipling, and good works, your LQ becomes manifested and real.

How does one become a butterfly? You must want to fly so much that you are willing to give up being a caterpillar. —Trina Paulus

How does one become a leader? You must want to lead so much that you are willing to give up being a follower. Are you ready?

STAGE 3 – LEADER

- *Description of your current circumstances: Success*

- *Your heart's cry: "I need more time to invest into my leaders!"*

- *Internal Questions: "How successful can we become? Do we need a bigger church, more staff, more marketing, and more etc.? Do we look successful?"*

- *Focus: Positive Self-Centered*

- *Action word to exiting this season: Successor*

Stage 2 is to be a great follower who models mastery at what you do. However, God doesn't want His followers to just follow Him; He wants you to eventually become a "fisher of men." God wants you to become a leader who influences others to do what is right and to do things with excellence. Only a few people (15 percent) reach the level of becoming a leader—but all can become leaders if willing to put in the effort. And the reward for climbing to this level gives you the crown of sweet success.

Success is never enough. Once you are at this level, you have to realize you have a good start, but you are not at the top of the mountain yet. And at the same time, you must realize it is not all about success. Leadership is never all about you; it's about others— preparing and equipping the people around you. You must develop a team who continually reproduces Christ-like leaders long after you graduate to heaven.

At this stage, we must be really honest with ourselves and admit that up to this point it has really all been about our own personal achievements, recognition, and desires for personal possessions. It takes a lot of humility and honesty to admit it. We can sometimes be self-deceived because we don't think we are self-centered.

The crown of success feels good for a season, but eventually a person reasons that there must be more. As a leader, you will experience success in life, but God doesn't want you to stop there.

Leaders reproduce leaders. The next step is to produce your successor. Leadership without a successor equals failure. So you are not really a good leader unless you take what is inside you and hand it off to the next generation through reproducing, not cloning.

STAGE 4 – PATRIARCH

- *Description of your current circumstances: Significance*

- *Your heart's cry: "Give me more children!"*

- *Internal Questions: "Did we really make any difference that will last? What difference will we be making one hundred years from now?"*

- *Focus: Other-Centered*

- *Action word to exiting this season: Legacy*

Over the years, we grow in wisdom and experience as we become spiritual fathers and mothers—patriarchs. This is the final step to reaching the summit on your journey to becoming everything God wants you to become. Only a minority of people, about 2 to 5 percent in the world, reach this top level of impact, influence, and income. At this stage, you are recognized as a leader of high level leaders. Your focus has shifted away from success. As Bob Buford has written, you move from *success to significance.*

The patriarch is at a place of maturity where he or she is standing at the top looking down the mountain—this person is fully committed to the success of others.

LQ Solution: The bookends of your life should not be the day you were born and the day you die.

Your life bookends were known by God before the foundations of the world. And He didn't intend your life to end at your death. Your life should carry on long after you die—through your spiritual and natural progeny. That is significance and legacy. Your goal: be part of something that outlives you.

I like what Paul Crouch, founder of TBN, said to his sons live on television, "I have legally seen to it that I will be running the ministry from the grave so nobody can sell the station and stop Christian television from being aired in the future."

The main reason I write books is to continue changing lives from my grave. People generally don't throw away books; they put them on their bookshelf, or they pass them on. So even when I am dead, I pray my books will scream out from someone's bookshelf, "Read me!" Then I will be helping people even after I am dead and gone. Significance and legacy are much more than being born and dying. Plan to make a difference that outlives you.

Where Are You?

The first question God asked Adam and Eve after the fall in their personal lives was, "Where are you?" He was not asking a geographical question. God did not ask this question because God could not find them, God wanted Adam and Eve to "self-discover." I hear God asking, "Why have you moved away from the place of leadership, confidence, and dominion and into this place of following, fear, and shame?"

As your coach, I want to help you get to where you really want to go. However, my first step is to help you discover where you really are.

Where are you? Meaning, what stage are you in at this time in your life on the *Leadership Advancement Mountain*? Check the appropriate box:

☐ Wanderer

☐ Follower

☐ Leader

☐ Patriarch

What is your next step?_____

_____

_____

What is your key action word for this season of your life?_____

_____

_____

Where Is Your Organization?

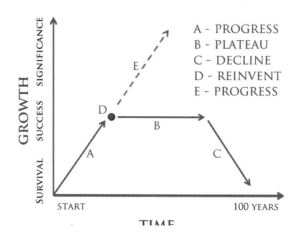

Figure 2
Organizational Progress Chart

As you study the organizational progress chart above, where is your church, business, or organization when you consider your current personal, numerical, and financial status? Check the appropriate boxes below.

Personal	Numerical	Financial
☐ A	☐ A	☐ A
☐ B	☐ B	☐ B
☐ C	☐ C	☐ C
☐ D	☐ D	☐ D
☐ E	☐ E	☐ E

The predictable journey for most organizations that end up in extinction follow this course or pattern:

A. The organization starts small with a leader who has a desire to solve a problem or meet a need. Finances are low. Dreams and passions are high. The organization experiences great struggles and hardships. Through persistence, progress creates the momentum needed and they eventually break out of survival and experience success.

B. The organization experiences a season of success and then continues to ride the wave, and managers maintain the status quo. Future becomes cloudy and passion runs low. No changes take place, and the organization starts to plateau.

C. Whatever is not evaluated, stagnates in time. Leaders and managers refuse to make improvements; gradually the organization starts to decline. The organization becomes irrelevant and eventually dies.

To take your organization to the next level and beyond, you must understand:

1. Success is temporary. An organization must evolve or die. Clarity is needed. Therefore, reinvention (D) is needed to move beyond success to creating an organization of significance (E).

2. Goodness is free, but greatness will cost you. The price of greatness is change. Most do not want to pay the price because change brings chaos. But without chaos, you have no progress.

Great leaders have the confidence to make changes before the organization starts to plateau. In order to keep up, you cannot let up. We must keep pushing ourselves up the leadership mountain to advance to the next level of our leadership quotient.

Everyone has three choices to make every day:

- Choice 1 – *Give up.*

- Choice 2 – *Give in.*

- Choice 3 – *Give it our all!*

When we choose to give it our all, we will live our lives happy and fulfilled at the end of our journey. As I said in Chapter One, every human being will have to face their own mortality someday. Before we die, we want to know that our life counted for something—that we made a difference in the world in some way.

Do you want your life to count—to make a difference?

Most people want to know that their lives impacted others significantly. Sooner or later we will be facing two graves. One is the Grave of Regret, which is where the person goes who never unleashed his or her full potential. The other is the Grave of Fulfillment—our highest and best destination! When we are a few moments away from our last breath, we can say, "I unleashed my potential in life. I made the difference that I was supposed to make here on this earth."

I want to rob the Grave of Regret from its power by helping you unleash your Leadership Quotient. The only way I can empower you to rob your Grave of Regret is by helping you maximize your full potential.

The leader inside you is screaming to get out—and today we are going to open that cage so that real leader will emerge. May I ask you: *How important is it to you that you become all that God has called you to be?* The insights presented in this book are all about keeping you from facing the Grave of Regret.

Unleash Your LQ

- What three changes in me would be most pleasing to God?

- How do I picture myself? Where am I on my journey up the mountain? What do I need to do next?

- Knowing that God has created me to be a leader, what will I do to prepare, train, and get equipped?

- What do I need to do or to think to move from Victim-ship to Leadership?

- How important is it to me to become all God has called me to be?

If the American church actually set out to do this "exploit" for God, bringing 20,000,000 to Christ this year, another 20,000,000 next year...in three or four years we wouldn't recognize our culture. Broadway and Hollywood would have to acknowledge the shift in audience preferences. Abortion clinics would wonder where all their customers went. Drug abuse would plummet. Some will accuse me of idealistic dreaming, but isn't this plan the last thing Jesus told us to fulfill before his ascension? "Go and make disciples of all nations," he said, "baptizing them in the name of the Father and of the Son and of the Holy Spirit, and teaching them to obey everything I have commanded you" (Matt. 28:19–20). What will it take to shake denominational leaders, pastors, and laypeople, seeing that we all must answer to Christ at the Judgment Seat one day? Our sense of inadequacy is no excuse, given that he has promised to work with us as we set our hearts to the task of extending his kingdom.

—Jim Cymbala and Dean Merrill,
Fresh Wind, Fresh Fire

CHAPTER THREE

ADVANCE

Leaders Are Agents of Improvement and Transformation

I like the marketing tagline for Lowe's Home Improvement Center—*Never Stop Improving.* In my mind, leaders keep things advancing. To advance simply means to move forward, to progress, and to bring improvement. Everyone has the ability to keep improving. To achieve greater impact, influence, and income in this century's global society, it is essential to keep pushing for *constant improvement.* I learned when I was speaking in Japan, that the Japanese called this process of advancement *kaizen.* This means that in order to be a world-class person, leader, or organization, everybody has to be thinking every day about ways to make everything better. In every sphere of society, there are demands for bigger, better, higher performance, and excellence.

More and more in years to come, successful churches, businesses, and organizations will be the ones best able to apply the creative energy of individuals toward constant improvement. However, constant improvement is a value that cannot be forced upon you or your organization. It has to come from you. The only way to get people to adopt constant improvement as a way of life is by setting a great example and by empowering them.

WANTED! Leaders

World-class leaders and elite performers are constantly asking themselves the following question: "Is the way I'm performing truly excellent and reflective of someone who is operating at a world-class standard?" We live in a world where mediocrity is the norm. So, when you truly devote yourself to becoming a leader of excellence in the way that you think and act, you stand out in a crowded marketplace. You show genuine leadership.

LQ Solution: You will be known for something at the end of your life. Pick it now. Some day_____(person/ organization) will be a world-class _____!

There is a critical need for leadership intelligence in the world. According to the National Leadership Index from the Harvard Kennedy School Center for Public Leadership, 68 percent of Americans believe that we are currently facing a leadership crisis.

Like an automatic machine gun, the media daily shoot story after story about how another major leader has failed to set a good example. The stories know no limits: politicians, CEOs, clergy, sports stars, entertainment celebrities, college coaches, bank presidents, brokers, and the list goes on and on. We continually hear how leaders valued their own financial prosperity and selfish ambitions more then the desires and needs of the constituency they serve. We need leaders today with greater confidence, competence, and character to improve our nation and world—to set positive examples and move us forward.

The world is in crisis! People are crying out for leaders. Who will lead us? Where are we headed? Is somebody going to do something? Who is going to step up to the challenges? Who has the answers to the problems we are facing?

LQ Solution: Spirituality is the foundation on which to build great nations, cultures, churches, and businesses.

Chick-fil-A organization's operational philosophy is built on biblical principles. Chick-fil-A founder Truett Cathy opened his first restaurant in 1946 and decided that the restaurant would not be open on Sundays. He has often shared that his decision was as much practical as spiritual. He believes that all of the Chick-fil-A operators and their employees should have an opportunity to rest, spend time with family and friends, and worship if they choose to do so. This is part of their recipe for success. Chick-fil-A has become the second largest quick-service chicken restaurant chain in the United States—with more than 1,400 franchises. In 2010, annual sales were over $3.5 billion.[1]

The United States was founded on God and Judeo-Christian principles. Our nation became the hub of wealth and prosperity because of operating with biblical truths. History has proven that good morals equal good economics. In crisis times, the church should be taking the lead, but we have taken a back seat! The world is no longer fighting us, they are ignoring us. Why? The church is full of intelligent but impoverished people. The answer is revealed in the ancient story about the poor wise man.

*There was a little city with few men in it; and a great king came against it, besieged it, and built great snares around it. Now there was found in it **a poor wise man**, and he by his wisdom delivered the city. Yet **no one remembered that same poor man**. Then I said: "Wisdom is better than strength. Nevertheless the poor man's wisdom is despised, And **his words are not heard**" (Ecclesiastes 9:14-16).*

The church has the wisdom of God for the solutions of all the problems the world is facing. Unfortunately, we do not have the financial wealth to back up what we have to say. The majority of Christian believers are simply followers in the marketplace. They are in survival mode. They have just enough to pay their bills. Most church members have not produced a life of success so the world looks at us and does not respect—or remember—what we have to say. Why? Because the church has become the poor wise man!

Leadership Intelligence Needed in the Church

I have reached the same conclusions as George Barna and John Maxwell in that the leadership vacuum in the church today arose during the twentieth century. Church expert and statistician George Barna asserts, "Leadership remains one of the glaring needs of the church. People are always willing to follow God's vision, but too frequently they have no exposure to either vision or true leadership." Just a few years ago, Barna penned some sobering conclusions based on his research: "After fifteen years of digging into the world around me, I have reached several conclusions regarding the future of the Christian Church in America. The central conclusion is that the American Church is dying due to lack of leadership…. Nothing is more important than leadership."

Without wise leadership, a nation falls; there is safety in having many advisers (Proverbs 11:14 NLT).

When Christ returned to heaven to sit on the right hand of His Father, He left His Church on earth to do work that has an eternal impact. If the local church isn't well-led, then the Kingdom of God suffers and will not be able to fulfill His mission for this generation.[2]

LQ Solution: Leaders have a responsibility to create a culture that encourages people to increase their leadership intelligence so they can maximize their potential and achieve a common team goal.

My Transition from Sinner to Minister to Leader

Today I am known as America's #1 Confidence Coach. However, my journey up the mountain of leadership did not start off well. At twenty-three, I was a professional sinner. I was John Travolta Junior, boogie-woogieing in the bars all night long. Back then I smoked, drank, sold drugs, and did drugs. I was a very successful sinner. However, I felt dirty inside, and I knew I wasn't right with God. I wanted forgiveness and a new life.

Then one night, a preacher really preached the gospel to me. He spoke about how Jesus loved me, would forgive my sin, and remove the feelings of shame and condemnation. I didn't turn my life over to God so He would make me a millionaire. I wanted the guilt and shame of my sin to vanish. I wasn't even trying to avoid hell because I wanted to go to heaven. For me, it was all about the forgiveness of sins. I was such a sinner that it was hard for me to believe God would forgive me and wipe my slate clean. When Jesus came into my life, my personal demons left me—alcohol, drugs, cussing, and chasing after every woman on the block. I was radically changed after giving my life to Christ.

A week later, during my devotional and prayer time, God called me into the ministry. I saw a vision of myself speaking to thousands of people. Here is where I had my first problem with God. We had a wrestling match over me becoming a minister. I flat out asked God if He was crazy. I told God that He obviously didn't understand what a sinner I had been. I kept thinking over and over again about all the terrible things I had done in the past. Then I realized that God had forgiven me and had already forgotten all my sins and lawless deeds.

LQ Solution: God does not consult your past to determine your future. God does not live in your past.

I went to my pastor and told him about my former life and how I turned my life over to Jesus Christ. I explained how I saw a vision of myself speaking to thousands of people, traveling the world, being on television, and writing many books. I was looking for a mature spiritual father, but ran into a genuine, modern-day religious Pharisee. My pastor basically told me I'd never amount to anything. He told me how he came from four generations of preachers. I felt disqualified because I came from four generations of alcoholics. He advised me to calm down, and just be a good little church member.

I left his office totally confused, thinking, *I'm not good enough to go into ministry. Maybe I should just keep doing what I'm doing.* My girlfriend, Bonnie (who is now my wife), was with me, and after we got into the car, she looked at me with fire in her eyes. She was so angry. She said she was never going back to that church again. Over the next few days, she convinced me that God could use my past in a powerful way to help other struggling people. She convinced me to go to Bible school.

After graduating from Bible school, I was excited, enthusiastic, and ready to preach. I prayed a stupid prayer and said, "God, I believe I can take Your Word and preach it right next door to hell and grow a great church." I should have prayed, "God please send me to Honolulu." God answered my prayer and sent me to a place out in the middle of nowhere in Central Florida. The town had one road, one flashing red light, and a post office. The community had become a virtual ghost town after a huge logging company harvested all the pine trees, leaving everybody in the area to live in abject poverty. I am talking about homes that didn't even have floors and had outhouses in the backyards.

The denomination I was part of at the time sent me to a sixty-seven-year-old, small, run-down, dying church with a membership of twenty senior citizen ladies. The church building looked more like a lean-to than a church. The first thing my wife said when we pulled into the parking lot was, "I'm not going in there. It looks like it may fall down on us." Because the district expected me to preach there that coming Sunday morning, she reluctantly agreed—if I promised to preach my fastest sermon and then get out of there quickly. I was only twenty-five at the time, and I preached to them about returning to their first love and getting on fire for God. I asked them why they had lost their zeal and let their hearts grow cold. I laid it out there and gave an altar call. They all responded to the altar call, and I was stunned.

Bonnie walked up to the platform and said, "The Lord showed me a picture of the Charlie Brown Christmas Tree." I was thinking that she ate too much pizza the day before, but she said, "God showed me that this church is like the Charlie Brown Christmas Tree. It was ugly and nobody else wanted any part of it, but we are going to take it and we are going to make it beautiful."

LQ Solution: Leaders are confident enough to take a mess and turn it into a message.

Something happened inside me that day. Destiny was downloaded into my heart. I was able to see something beyond what my natural eyes could see. I saw the church changing and the entire community revitalized. I was so excited and ready to take on the responsibility of growing this church. I knew inside and believed with every cell of my body that I could be used by God to change this community for the better. I took responsibility that day and agreed to be their pastor.

LQ Solution: True leadership requires the leader to take responsibility for leading followers into the exciting unknown and creating a new reality for them.

Here is my definition of the ingredients needed in the "leadership process" to turning your dreams into reality:

Leadership Process Defined:

The deposit of destiny in the heart of a person to solve a problem or meet a need that gives birth to a crystal clear purpose, organized and focused by a strategic plan, measured by priorities and goals, ignited by a passion that is highly inspirational, producing the result of influencing people to get involved in making a change that benefits all of humankind.

Leadership Is a Result

A careful study of this definition reveals that leadership is not a title, pursuit, method, or theory—it is an end result. The end result is produced by people being influenced to help all humankind. Under this definition, the word *leader* is not a label that you give yourself. Leader is what the people call you who are inspired, motivated, and ultimately influenced because they are stirred to participate in the positive vision of the destiny that you are presenting them—whether it is the vision or destiny for a country, business, church, company, or cause. Whether it is Jesus Christ, Mother Teresa, Martin Luther King Jr., Nelson Mandela, or the president of the United States, they all went through this leadership process in order to influence others to make a difference in their generation.

LQ Solution: Inspirational and motivational leadership is in. Dictatorship and positional leadership is out. Leaders inspire and never force others to follow.

A further study of this definition also reveals the importance of inspiration and motivation produced by destiny in the heart of a leader. True leadership is influence through inspiration. If you desire to become a leader of influence and transformation, you must be able to answer these two questions: "How do I inspire others?" and "What is the fuel of my inspiration?"

Leaders Inspire through Their Passion

The source of inspiration is passion—a passion that is ignited by a sense of destiny and purpose to change the world that is beyond the borders of self and personal gain. Leadership passion is birthed from a destiny and purpose that is not just something to live for, but also to die for.

How does a person inspire others? A leader inspires by communicating a crystal clear destiny, purpose, and strategic plan for the future. Destiny and purpose unlock a leader's passion. Leaders can effectively express their inner passions, which find a common purpose in the hearts of others. Passion in the heart of the leader attracts people to take action to achieve the desired results.

Growing churches and organizations have people who really want to be involved. It's not the product or service you are providing, stock options, fringe benefits, or the salary that attract great people. Great people are attracted because they want to become part of an organization that is going somewhere, that is doing something, that is changing the world.

LQ Solution: Focusing on the organization's leadership process, not its packaging, attracts new people.

Apple's cofounder, Steve Jobs, was trying to convince John Sculley to leave his job as senior vice president of PepsiCo to become the CEO of Apple. Sculley wasn't particularly interested in leaving a secure position at Pepsi to run this brand-new company. Jobs changed that by asking him, "Do you want to spend the rest of your life selling sugared water or do you want a chance to change the world?" Being part of a company that was doing something important is what attracted John Sculley to Apple.[3]

I passionately stood up on the first day as the pastor of that little church and boldly told the entire congregation that we were going to revitalize the entire community. I explained how the Bible tells us we are to go into all the world and preach the gospel—and we were going to do just that. I told them how I could see the church totally full and our entire community being changed. I set focus and priorities. I pointed out that there was an equal number of black, white, and Hispanic people living in our area and challenged them to reach out to everybody in the area. I had a massive action plan for our all-white congregation. I told them we would start in the black community and go house to house. I explained that it was easy for us to love and reach out to people who were like us, but we needed to reach out and love people who were not like us. I asked for their help and commitment.

You won't believe what happened. It was amazing! That little church went from twenty people all the way down to five in the next six months. Three of them were my wife, daughter, and myself—the other two were a young couple who had come to work with us. I discovered that nobody was interested in reaching out to unsaved people, especially the black community. When the people left the church, our financial support left with them. I was left with a run-down church, no people, and now no money. Things were not looking good.

I must admit, I was totally shocked by the prejudice and the immaturity of supposedly seasoned Christian people. I learned that day that longevity does not mean maturity. Despite the external death threats from the Ku Klux Klan and internal church opposition, we determined that we were not going to stay stuck within the four walls of the church. My revelation was bigger than my situation. We boldly went outside the church and did raw evangelism. We knocked on every door of the hundred or so homes in that community. We started winning people to Jesus Christ and built the first multicultural church in the region. An amazing thing happened; that church grew bigger than the community it dwelled in. Successful? Perhaps. Significant? Not even.

LQ Solution: Maximizing your influence, impact, and income requires you to transition from a minister mind-set to a leader mind-set.

I had started following Christ, pastoring a church, and preaching great sermons, but now the process of becoming a leader had to begin. Because there was a demand placed on my inner leader, I had demonstrated some Leadership Quotient; but a significant thing happened to me at this level that started a transformation in me.

But before I go into that, several myths must be debunked before you can journey with me into significant, servant leadership that maximizes your impact, influence, and income as you *discover, increase, and maximize your Leadership Quotient.* The next chapter deals with alignment—and reveals how to transition your mind-set.

Unleash Your LQ

- What in your past is limiting your future? Will you release it?

- Do you have the confidence to take any mess you or others have created in your church and develop a plan for change and transformation?

- What is your core message or vision for the future for yourself and those you are leading?

- As you transition from a minister to a leader mind-set, what new picture must be drawn in your mind so you see yourself for what you are becoming?

Endnotes

1. http://www.chick-fil-a.com/Company/Highlights-Fact-Sheets; accessed February 27, 2012.
2. *John Maxwell's Leadership Bible,* Introduction, (Nashville, TN: Thomas Nelson, 2002).
3. Samuel R. Chand, *Ladder Shifts,* (Huntley, IL: Mall Publishing Company, 2006), 15.

When Kurt Senske was only thirty-six years old, he took over leadership of a company that was losing money rapidly. Yet in only three years, he pulled together a team that turned the company around. The key to their success? "We followed sound Christian leadership strategies that included incorporating the principles of servant leadership from the bottom up, creating a healthy culture that valued its employees."

What is a servant leader? It is someone who, in Senske's words, refuses to use people as means to an end—who always asks, "Am I building people up, or am I building myself up and merely using those around me?" A servant leader creates an atmosphere of "transparency" in which all relevant information is shared openly, so that everyone has an opportunity to make responsible decisions. Finally, a servant leader lets go of command-and-control methods, and creates a culture that allows everyone to grow into leaders, stretching their own God-given talents.

–Nancy Pearcey and Phillip E. Johnson
Total Truth

CHAPTER FOUR

ALIGNMENT

Leaders Improve Mind-sets, Skill Sets, and Assets

Before speaking at secular business events or on television, I am often introduced as a motivational speaker. I am much more than a motivational speaker who excites an audience to a temporary emotional high. In fact, I prefer not to be called a motivational speaker. Why? If my only goal is to motivate people, I may be just motivating them to keep doing stupid things faster.

Rather, I think of myself as a professional communicator and inspirational teacher who helps people unlearn wrong belief systems, pushes them beyond their perceived limitations, helps people see what is missing, and challenges them to better their best so they can get quick results in a short amount of time.

When I start the first session of my leadership conferences I ask the crowd, "How many of you came to learn something today?" Almost 100 percent of the crowd raise their hands and enthusiastically say, "Yes!"

Then I say, "That is your problem! It's not what you need to learn today that is going to help you change your life. It is what you need to UNLEARN. Debunking untruths will unshackle you and allow you to achieve what you really want. It's time to unlearn myths and misconceptions and align yourself with what's real and true."

When we align ourselves with something or someone, we position that thing or person for proper performance. For instance, suppose one of your car's front tires was out of alignment. How would this one tire affect the handling performance of your car? The car would pull to the left or the right causing all the other wheels to perform below their maximum potential. The one out-of-line tire affects the performance and outcome of the rest of the car. This is what happens when belief systems about leadership are out of alignment.

This chapter will help you get all your wheels—mind-sets, skill sets, and assets—in alignment by identifying six myths people believe about leadership. As a leader, you and your organization must be empowered to operate at peak performance, and knowing these six myths will change your mindset.

Please don't be deceived; the tire that is out of alignment will not self-correct! Wrong belief systems don't change automatically. Changes must be intentionally made. Many leaders tend to ignore problem people and poor performing departments that are out of alignment and hope, wish, and pray that things will just "work out in time." Over the past sixteen plus years of helping leaders, I have found that the tire actually gets worse over time and so does the performance of departments that are out of alignment. I am sure you have found that when one leader is out of alignment, the rest of the organization is affected.

Unlearn Myths about Leadership!

Our first step together to develop your Leadership Quotient is to debunk the myths that have been keeping your LQ in an undeveloped, immature state. There is truth; truth is real and reliable, working for all people at all times and in all situations. Real truth springs from the nature and person of God who is truth (see Psalm 31:5). Then there's myth; myth is conventional wisdom that may work for some people, some time, and in some situations.

Let me help you demythologize what you may have erroneously thought to be real but simply isn't!

Myth #1
The size of the church determines the level of success.

LQ Solution: Success is measured by significance and impact—not by size!

I have spoken at hundreds of churches all around the globe. I have been to small churches to some of the largest churches in the world. Some small churches justify their small numbers with the thought that they are the "only" church in the area really preaching the Bible. Therefore, because they are small, this is proof that God is happy with them. In fact, many are small because the church lacks direction, the building needs renovating, the music is outdated, the sermons are irrelevant, boring, and too long—and quite frankly, the congregation is unfriendly to visitors who come to the church for the first time. The good news to the small church pastor, all these things can be changed.

On the other side of the coin, we may be tempted to believe that if the church has thousands of people, its mega size portends mega success. Let me challenge you with this; at that little church I first pastored, we saw almost 50 percent of the people in our community come to Christ. When we first arrived, the church and community were totally run down. We painted, repaired, and fixed up our church. Then we saw to it that every house on the road had a fresh coat of paint, was repaired, and refreshed. Isn't that awesome? That small town's community was transformed, and the culture of that region began to change.

Through preaching the gospel, we empowered the people who lived there to get jobs, start their own businesses, and change their lives for the better. Before hearing the good news of the gospel, the people were hopeless and living off welfare.

LQ Solution: The success of a church is not determined by the number of people who attend; it is determined by the condition of the culture, the region in which it dwells.

This means you can have a ten-or-10,000 member church, but if the culture surrounding that church is "going to hell," is it really a success in God's eyes? Here's the truth: *The way you create heaven on earth is to depopulate hell.* The goal is to have more people going to heaven than going to hell. A smaller church can possibly be a bigger success at 150 members than a pastor with 10,000 if his community is not being changed.

Never judge a leader's success or a church's success based on the number of people who attend. Let the yardstick be the condition of the surrounding community. The question really is, "Are we making the region that God has planted us in better?"

Myth #2
To build a bigger church I have to work harder as a pastor.

LQ Solution: Growth and health happen when the pastor transitions from a minister mind-set to a leader mind-set.

When the church I pastored reached about 150 people, I was presented with a huge problem. I had lots of passion and energy, but absolutely no wisdom. Isn't it interesting that the older we get the more wisdom we acquire through experience—but the less energy we have? I was really busy, because I had the mentality of being a "super pastor." I had the philosophy that it's all about a one-man show. I set up my church as The Keith Johnson Show; and, of course, I was the featured star.

- Healing needed? I was God's man of faith and power to pray for healing.

- Someone sick in the hospital? Super Keith showed up at the hospital.

- A dysfunctional person needed help? Pastoral counselor Keith to the rescue.

- Who was available to turn on the lights and heat? Pastor Keith was.

- Sound system broken? Keith the music man to the rescue.

Leader Keith had to be the one to do everything. Super Keith was running around like crazy and with 150 people in the congregation, my time was maxed out. I remember going to the church one day and looking at my appointment calendar. At lunchtime there was a name written in bold letters that went all the way across the page—**Bonnie Johnson.** It was circled and highlighted. When I saw that my wife had to make an appointment with me for lunch, I knew I was in big trouble.

I went to lunch with my wife that day, and she said, "You know you are real spiritual, but you don't know how to lead at all. I know a woman pastor not far from here who is really passionate about raising up leaders. I'd like you to meet this woman pastor."

Alarms went off in my head as my wife said "woman pastor." Back then, I had what I call a George Jefferson, Fred Sanford, Archie Bunker mentality—the three stooges of male chauvinism. They were my only role models. I believed the only things women were good for was birthing children, making meals, and ironing clothes. A woman pastor was not even on my radar, but my wife was really agitated with me, so I agreed.

By the way, you can learn my fourteen Bible proofs that God uses women in ministry and leadership in my book or training class in Destiny College titled *Women in Ministry and Leadership.* Reluctantly, off I went to a large leadership conference this woman pastor was hosting. As I sat there waiting for the scheduled worship team to begin, I spotted a lady. She was doing absolutely nothing. People were graciously serving her and taking care of things. I sat there scratching my head wondering, *I can't even get two people to help me with anything at the church.* An interesting thought crossed my mind just about the time the music started, *Maybe I'm doing something wrong.*

Suddenly this lady gets up, points right at me, and says, "You sir, you're a great minister. But, you are a poor leader. God has a great destiny for your life. You are going to lead other leaders, but you have got to first learn how to become a leader."

There was no doubt in my mind that God was speaking to me through this woman. When God wants to change your life, He has to offend your mind. At every defining moment in my life, I had the opportunity to be offended when someone taught, trained, or sought to equip me. But as I evaluated what I was told, I realized that I really needed that equipping or educational experience.

When I left the conference, I shook her hand and said, "Thank you for that word. I didn't like it, but it challenged me." She said, "Here young man, here's a tape."

She gave me a tape by pastor, author, and equipper John Maxwell. I had never heard of him before, but I listened to the tape in the car as I drove home with my wife. What he said changed my life and was the key factor I needed to maximize my impact, influence, and income. I discovered that to move from where I was to where I needed to go required me to increase my LQ. I needed to start reading more books about leadership, listening to more CDs, and begin to develop myself as a leader in a greater way. That is the only way we can be ready for the next level that God has for us. Every new level demands a better way of thinking and working.

Being a good pastor doesn't necessarily translate into being a good leader. Also, being a highly spiritual marketplace person does not translate into being a good leader. I kept hearing these words over and over again, "Transition from a minister to a leader." I was an expert at doing church, but I wasn't really an expert at the art of influencing people and changing people's lives.

LQ Solution: Commit yourself to the process of transforming yourself from being just a minister to becoming a servant leader.

Making a difference in the marketplace and our communities is our challenge. It takes a totally different level of thinking to walk the halls of government or participate in boardroom discussions of Fortune 500 companies than it takes to walk the halls to the church office. It takes a whole different level of thinking to operate and communicate in a church service versus communicating in a secular environment. Many times, congregants have higher levels of expertise and education—and they judge every word the pastor says.

The End Result—What Are You Producing?

When I help pastors set up the proper structure for church growth, the number one problem we run into is finding enough quality people to get the job done. The cry of most pastors: "I need leaders to help me!" We must take a serious look at the entire process of what happens to people when they come into our churches as a wanderer and then what happens to them once they are immersed into the culture of our church. What kind of person do they become after a year on the other side? Church member? Follower? Leader?

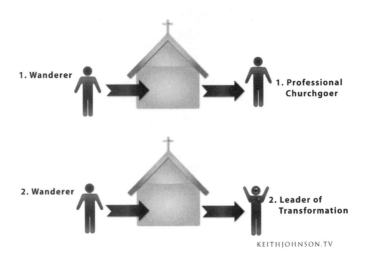

The questions are:

- What are we building?

- Are we building wimps or warriors?

- Are we building lions or pussycats?

- Are we building people of mental toughness or weak-minded quitters?

- Are we developing winner or losers?

- Are we building people who are problem solvers or people who run from problems?

- Are we building professional churchgoers or leaders of transformation?

In my humble opinion, we have created professional churchgoers, but we have not created leaders of transformation. We are great at creating followers, but we are poor at developing leaders in the marketplace. Only 2 percent of the people who attend church services ever become full-time ministry workers. Most church members spend two to four hours in church a week and then spend fifty or more hours in the marketplace. Therefore, 98 percent of the people who walk through the doors of our churches are working outside the four walls of the church in government, business, education, media, and the arts. We must be strategic and intentional in creating a culture by setting up systems within the church to automatically produce leaders.

LQ Solution: If you are serious about cultural transformation, focus on building professional leaders of transformation instead of professional churchgoers.

I believe the level of spiritual understanding in today's churches far exceeds that of any other generation. We have more Bible knowledge today than the great men and women of God of old, in that we have the benefit of centuries of insights from many, many great men and women of God. We may know a lot about spirituality, but not a whole lot about being leaders. This is why we have failed to change the culture. Now is the time to transition from a minister mind-set to a leader mind-set.

Myth #3
Only some people are called to be leaders.

LQ Solution: The DNA for leadership comes from Christ's nature in every believer.

No doubt you have heard it said that, "Some people are called to lead—only some." I certainly believe that is true for the majority of the people in the world who have not received God's DNA. However, when you become part of the Kingdom of God, the Father's call to greatness goes out to everyone. Although the call to leadership goes out to everyone, few accept the challenge to become the people they are supposed to become.

Actually, it is easy to become a leader today because so few people have the confidence to step up to the plate and lead. Remember, God's Overall Desire (G.O.D.) is for you to be on top; we are the head and not the tail.

For way too long, the church has been a magnet for attracting losers not winners, victims not victors. "If you are really messed up, just come and be part of us" has been our evangelistic strategy. Yet, God says the manifestation of the blessings of God is that we are on the top not on the bottom.

The church should be the incubator that develops world-class leaders who produce extraordinary results. It is not our "Jesus in our hearts" Christian bumper stickers or our T-shirts with crosses and scriptures on them that are going to draw the world to us. The new evangelistic thrust must be the world seeing our good works and glorifying our God in heaven (read Matthew 5).

Hidden within every follower is a leader waiting to emerge. The real you hasn't come to the surface yet. God has placed you here on this planet to lead something, somebody. Everybody is called to become a leader. Christ's description of leadership was "making disciples." You might say, "If everybody is born to lead, then who is going to follow?" We start by following, being servants and disciples, and then becoming leaders who reproduce themselves.

Myth #4:
Let's find out what people want and give it to them. Make them feel good.

LQ Solution: Real leaders are change agents.

We are called to be leaders of transformation. If we look closely, we can easily observe that the church has failed at transforming our culture. Truthfully, the church has been enculturated! The culture seems to be transforming the church. As a sound bite—the divorce rate in the church is the same as, and has sometimes exceeded, that of society! This is the church's fault; we have failed to make a difference, to be different. We have produced "professional churchgoers" instead of leaders of transformation. The church is full of spiritual people who are managers of the status quo, followers of the ordinary—but few are true leaders.

Leaders bring change. Even though I was only twenty-three years of age, I did something right in the first church I pastored. The church was in crisis. I didn't just try and make those twenty elderly women feel good during church services. I came in as a change agent and led them into a process of change. Admittedly, I did a lot of things wrong, but I also had the guts to do some things right. It takes guts to get out of ruts.

Most leaders today either make the mistake of becoming a manager of the status quo or they make too many changes too quickly. Making radical changes should be a strategic process. I have seen pastors make radical changes and lose half their church membership because they are without a coach and a strategic plan. Over the past sixteen years, I have helped many leaders make necessary transitions, with only a few casualties, so the organization experienced growth instead of decline.

Three Types of Leaders

There are three types of leaders:

1. *Carrot Heads* are weakened by the environment. If you take a pot of boiling water and stick a carrot in the water, the water changes the carrot. The carrot goes from strong to soft. In the heat of the environment, carrot head leaders become soft. The environment changes the leader instead of the leader changing the environment.

2. *Egg Heads* become hard inside due to the environment. When you put an egg in boiling water, the water causes the egg to get hard from the inside out. Instead of staying strong and bringing change to the environment, these leaders allow the environment to make them bitter and hard inside. The change agent's message will always be attacked by someone. It is tough not to become bitter when the ones who stab you in the back are the ones sitting in the congregation.

3. *Coffee Beans* under pressure change the environment. When you put coffee beans under the pressure of grinding and then into boiling water, the water doesn't change the coffee. The coffee changes the taste, smell, and composition of its environment. Whatever your environment, you need to become a leader who makes it better because you are there. We have to create leaders who are going to bring change into whatever culture they are immersed.[2]

Ultimately a genuine leader is not a searcher for consensus, but a molder of consensus. –Dr. Martin Luther King Jr.

LQ Solution: See yourself as a thermostat that brings change to the temperature of the room instead of a thermometer that adjusts with the temperature of the room.

The Seven Mountains of Your Culture

Every nation has a culture. Every region has a culture. Every business has a culture. Every church has a culture. In order to change the culture of a nation or region, we need to understand the key spheres in that culture. The culture is shaped by the belief systems of the people in that region or in the organization. Belief systems create behaviors, and the behaviors of a group of people create a culture. So in order to change a culture, we don't start out attacking the culture. We have to start by changing the people's fundamental belief systems. To change a belief system we have to repeat the teachings over and over until they become more than just a belief, they become part of their psyche or attitude.

We start changing a culture by teaching and changing the mind of that culture's members. Repetition is the mother of change—and that takes time. So whether you are a leader in business or church, never teach something just one time. Keep teaching it until it becomes part of their attitude and they start modeling it in their behavior.

There are seven key areas—many today call them cultural mountains—that shape culture in every nation. I believe that God wants us to change and transform these seven areas:

1. Religion
2. Family
3. Government
4. Business
5. Education
6. Media
7. Arts

The only possible way to change these mountains is for the church to focus our planning and efforts on developing and training future leaders to influence and impact each cultural mountain.

Myth #5:
Some people are just natural leaders.

LQ Solution: We learn leadership and develop as leaders as the mind of Christ shapes our actions and attitudes.

Most of us have not had good role models, so we have to be taught. Leadership is a skill that can and must be learned.

LQ Solution: Leadership is caught and taught. Catch it! Learn it!

Leaders don't come out of the womb being leaders. I believe leadership is both caught and taught. For example, my father belonged to the Satan's Escorts motorcycle club. Consequently, I had no role model from whom to catch leadership principles—I had to be taught. I went to school and earned a Master's in Christian Leadership. I also read and studied more than 125 books focused on leadership; my leadership quotient increased dramatically. In other words, I had self-motivation to be a leader. I had to start by reading and listening to those who had already made the transition from minister to leader. I went from a church that changed the culture to teaching others around the world what we did to grow a church bigger than the community in which it was located.

Five years from now, you'll be the same person you are today except for the people you meet, the books you read, and the CDs you listen to. —John Maxwell

Leader John Kelly became my spiritual father; we started traveling together. I noticed John living out many leadership principles almost intuitively. I would say things like, "John, you just demonstrated the law of the lid or the law of the hamburger" (more about these in Chapter Four). He would just look at me and say, "What are you talking about?" I had a hard time understanding why he didn't know what I was talking about. Then I found out that John was raised in a home where his father was a leader; he had built some of the largest bridges in America. John was raised by a father who modeled leadership inside and outside the home on a daily basis. Leadership principles that are caught are learned through example, experience, mentoring and coaching. It's a process of maturation, impartation, and influence rather than instruction and information.

Some people find themselves in a family, school, or cultural environment that immerses them in leadership experiences. Others must diligently seek education and instruction to be taught leadership. John Kelly was fortunate to have leadership modeled by his father continually so he "caught it."

Undertake something that is difficult; it will do you good. Unless you try to do something beyond what you have already mastered, you will never grow. –Ronald E. Osborn [2]

The majority of people in the world are not raised or surrounded by leaders. This is why it can seem like leaders are "born naturally," when in reality they have either caught it or have been taught it.

LQ Solution: You learn leadership through mentorship or mistakes, people or pain. Pay any price to be in the presence of a great leader.

Here is the wonderful reality. The more time I spend with John Kelly, the more I discover how I am growing as a "caught it" leader. At times, when I am helping leaders, I can hear him say things in my mind before I say them. Pay any price to get into the presence of great leaders—catch it and learn it!

I am impressed with the price paid by Tim Tebow, former Florida Gators quarterback now playing professional football. Living only an hour and a half away from Gator country, I must admit I have been a Tebow fan for many years. There is no argument that Tim Tebow understands how to maximize impact, influence, and income. His life made a difference on the Gators team, and now he is making a difference in the National Football League.

As spiritual people, we can be tempted to think that Tim's achievement is all about "God blessing him." There is no doubt in my mind that God has been doing that, but Tim has also been doing his part to maximize his potential so he can manifest his inner leader in the culture of the NFL.

I was watching a special on ESPN about Tim Tebow and how hard he had to work to improve his throwing style. The show explained the amount of time Tebow put in to preparing for his successful season with intense training, coaching, running, weight lifting, and throwing the football. At the end of the show, Tebow made the following comment: "Every day I ask myself, is there anybody else in this league who is working as hard as I am?" Then he said, "Most days, I don't think so. I want to work harder than any other person in the whole league."

Here is the coaching question I asked myself after the show, "Am I the hardest working speaker/leadership coach in the world?" Most days, I don't think so. Not even close. Then I asked myself this powerful question, "Am I working hard in preseason when nobody is watching me so my performance can be outstanding when opportunity knocks on my front door?" How would you answer these questions? Demonstrating your inner leader by being the best at what you do will take an inner determination to push yourself beyond the norm.

LQ Solution: Leaders first act in the natural, so God can give them SUPER-natural results.

Myth #6:
I need a title to lead.

LQ Solution: Developing LQ requires transition not position. There must be a transition from ignorance, laziness, and "stinking thinking" to awareness, knowledge, learning, and hard work.

A leader is simply a person who has decided to reach for more than the average person. Average is common. The majority of people on earth live average lives. So a leader is an average man or woman who decides to improve his or her lot in life. After you have made improvements, average people look up to you, want to follow you, want to become you, and will respect you. In that dynamic, if you become the best at what you do, you don't need a title because people will automatically want to follow you.

Have you ever attended a church where everyone seems to have a title? Minister so and so, Prophet or Prophetess Talk a Lot, Elder this or Deacon that…everyone has a title. Titles are often the incubators for those who are insecure. When people have to say their title to confirm their leadership, they are not the leaders they think they are.

Leadership is not about a title. You can be a housekeeper at a hotel; and if you decide to do your best by going in early, leaving late, going beyond the routine cleaning, and having a professional attitude—I guarantee that you will climb to the top. Your supervisor and others will notice you and you will be promoted. You made an impact, and eventually you will have more influence and income than the others. Wherever you are right now, you can climb to the top and be a leader.

Whatever your church assignment, make a quality decision to become the very best the church has ever had. If you do a little bit more than the average person, you will climb to the top and people will look up to you, respect you, and want to be who you are. That's leading without a title.

Everyone has two choices—to become more or less. Every day you have a choice. Am I going to read more or am I going to read less? Will I study a little more or a little less? Am I going to exert more effort or less? You make that choice every day of your life whether you realize it or not. So choose to become more. Then you will begin to lead without needing someone to call you by a certain title.

Realize that our example either helps people or hurts people. We are influencing people all the time—either negatively or positively. Our example affects people around us.

- Leadership is not about titles and positions.
- Leadership is about influencing others to do what is right.

Myth #7
I have to be perfect to be a leader.

LQ Solution: I will build on my strengths, stop condemning my weaknesses, and affirm the Leadership Quotient birthed in me by becoming a new creation in Christ.

When I was growing up, there was a big Bible on the coffee table in the living room, but I never saw anyone in my family ever reading or even touching it. In my mind, the Bible was God. When I would come in late at night drunk or stoned out of my mind, I had to go past the living room to get to my bedroom. I would intentionally stay as far away from that Bible as I possibly could. I didn't want God to know I was wasted.

After my radical conversion, something inside of me said, "I want to read that Bible." I will never forget the day I opened that Bible and a couple of cockroaches and spiders came out of it. I decided I wanted to read that Bible because I wanted to learn about some of the people in it. I thought the people in the Bible were all like Mother Teresa—perfect people.

As I began reading from the beginning, I came across Abraham, the "father of faith." I instantly discovered he had a lying problem. He told a king that his wife was his sister. Then I came to Moses. Now when I was a sinner, my picture of Moses was Charlton Heston with long, grey hair holding his rod over the Red Sea as it parted. As I read about Moses, I realized that he had major problems—including a bad temper, which made him a murderer.

When I was a little boy, I heard about David in Sunday school. He was a "man after God's own heart." Surely this guy had it together. But when I started reading about David, I found that, in modern-day terms, he watched pornography and cheated on his wife. I don't think that was the first time that David went up on the roof to watch nude Bathsheba taking a shower, do you? I am sure she took a shower at about the same time every day. People don't act on something the first time they think about it. People act on what they have thought about over and over. In modern days, David might well have gone on the Internet looking at pornography.

Struggling to find perfect leaders in the Old Testament, I thought, *Maybe I can find more perfect leaders in the New Testament because they were around Jesus.* As I randomly read through different books of the Bible, I met a man named Thomas. He had a major doubting problem. He was so negative that if he touched a battery it would go dead! All of the disciples seemed to have character flaws. I discovered that biblical leaders were human beings with issues—just like me.

No one other than Jesus is perfect. I have issues, and my life isn't perfect. My thought life is not perfect. My marriage isn't perfect. Although I am messed up, God is still using me. Everyone has issues, but do not allow them to hold you back. You can grow into the leader God wants you to become—starting right where you are today.

Focusing on your imperfections destroys your confidence and will wipe you out as a leader. —John P. Kelly

Don't buy into the myth that you have to be perfect to be in leadership. Trust me, every leader has clay feet. If you think you have to be perfect to lead, you will never step into the leadership role that God has called you to. Once you take off these limiting belief systems, you can begin moving toward the leader God has called you to be.

Myth #8:
An anointed, superspiritual, and loving pastor can grow a big church.

LQ Solution: My goal is to create a leadership culture by growing myself and building big people into their leadership potential through Christ.

Many people think that in order to grow a big church they need more anointing or more spiritual warfare; they need to fast and pray 24/7, be more gifted, or have a more charismatic personality. If this was the formula for successful church growth, then 80 percent of the churches in America should be large, not stuck at eighty people. On the other hand, there are a few (2 percent) huge churches that have leaders who don't pray, have extramarital affairs, don't love people, have no personality, and yet appear to be doing great.

I think the most important key to church health and growth lies in the leader's ability to grow his or her leadership skills.

Notice I did not say to grow his or her level of spirituality. I have found that the majority of megachurch pastors are people of character and sincerely love God and people, but they have a greater understanding of the importance of developing their own leadership competence and their teams.

LQ Solution: A leader's personal leadership growth determines the growth of the church's leadership team. The combined growth of the team determines the organization's growth.

The growth of an organization starts with the growth of the leader, but those around the leader have to grow too. I found that even if the leader grows, has wonderful leadership skills, lots of charisma and wisdom, but doesn't train, equip, disciple, coach and develop leaders around him or her, the organization is stuck in one place—stagnant. I know of thousands of leaders around the world who have the ability to pastor thousands of people—but the people around them aren't growing.

Every person on the team has to have a desire and determination to grow their LQ. I can teach you how to become a millionaire. I can teach you how to be a leader. I can teach you how to prosper and give you all the right tools. But you have to bring desire and determination to the table. I cannot put those ingredients for success in your heart. The entire team must have the desire to become something more than what they are, or you and the organization will be stuck.

Are You Willing to Change?

It's possible that there are people in your church or ministry who are stuck in one or more of these leadership myths. If so, a change must be made in order to move forward and go to the next level. As a leader, you have to become a myth-buster. You have a responsibility to grow your team. Are you willing to debunk your myths and change the mind-sets of those around you?

Leaders who reproduce leaders empower people to grow and maximize their leadership quotient.

When you change, some people from your past cannot or will not go with you into your future. Are you ready for change? If so, we can now turn to particular laws of leadership that will help you change your attitudes and actions.

Unleash Your LQ

- Seek out people who will mentor, disciple, and coach you in leadership skills. Make a list of people you will ask to mentor and coach you.

- Change your mind-set. Identify the myths about leadership you cling to and release them. Decide to let the truths about leadership set you free from church or cultural myths.

- Observe people who are teachable and desiring to become leaders. Make a list of these potential leaders and pray for God to guide you in ways to teach, train, motivate, and equip them.

- Buy copies of *The LQ Solution* for each team member. Use this book as your training manual.

- Determine to read, study, learn, and grow in leadership. With Destiny College, you can earn a Master's in Christian Leadership degree. *(See Appendix D.)*

Endnotes

1. John Mason, *Believe You Can—The Power of a Positive Attitude* (Kindle Edition), 69.
2. Part of a live keynote address presented by Brian Klemmer.

Leadership Is

Leadership is:

Knowing WHAT to do next...

Knowing WHY that is important...and,

Knowing HOW to bring the appropriate resources to bear on the need at hand.

Management is:

Maximizing time, energy, and money.

A leader has to manage—and—a manager has to lead.

Every day you are both leading and managing, regardless which activities you prefer!

—Bobb Biehl

CHAPTER FIVE

AXIOM

Leaders Know the WHAT, WHY, and HOW

I love reading the number one best seller of all times—the Bible. When I was new to the ministry, I heard a preacher boldly declare, "All you need to read is the Bible. Everything you need to know can be found in the Bible. That is the only book you need to read. The B-I-B-L-E...that's the book for me." The message sounded good and received an enthusiastic response from the crowd. Everybody in the church instantly shouted "Amen!" I thought, *Wow! This sounds pretty spiritual.* So I decided to make this same statement myself years ago to get the crowds to shout "Amen!" to me. However, I have changed my beliefs.

I have found that there are some truths about life, achievement, leadership, church growth, and business where the Bible is completely silent. I believe God wants us to learn some things experimentally. For instance, if you want to grow your church or organization through social network marketing, you cannot go to the Bible and find out how to set up a Facebook, YouTube, and Twitter account. If you want to learn as a pastor how to get your church on the first page of a Google search when somebody types in "local churches" for your area, you cannot go to the Bible and find information about Search Engine Optimization. You can learn about it, however, in my coaching program. There are principles you need to learn that are not in the Bible.

However, there are axioms or truths that are self-evident. They are laws that can produce predictable outcomes.

Axioms—Truths That Are Self-Evident

When a leader lives life by truths, principles, and laws, knowing what to do next and why it is important and how to get the resources to make it happen will become second nature.

Bobb Biehl taught me these three Ps for leadership:

- Priority – What do I need to do next?

- Principles – Why is this important?

- Plan – How do I get the resources to solve the problem or meet the need?

Success leaves clues. If you want to build a successful church, business, or university, you do not have to reinvent the wheel. Just find some proven laws that brought others success and they will bring you successful results also. Leadership laws and principles must take root in your thoughts and actions in order to grow yourself and others in leadership. Here are three essential laws of leadership I learned to develop and grow my own leadership quotient: The Law of Leadership Potential; the Law of the Lid; the Law of Quality. Let's look in detail at these laws.

1. The Law of Leadership Potential

An organization will only grow to the threshold of the combined leadership capacity within the organization. Our potential is enlarged or limited by the quality of leaders around us. A leader can have great potential, but can be limited by the quality of his team members.

We must evolve or die. The great enemy to change is complacency. Many leaders in organizations stop growing once they get a "position" or "title." Before they received the title they were doing great. Once they are in the position, they think they have arrived and can stop striving. One of my jobs as a coach is to get you and the organization to see what the reality of your current situation really is. Here is a coaching exercise I give to leaders to help everybody on the team realize they all need personal development.

What is your leadership potential?

Circle the number of people you think you have the potential to lead effectively.

2   5   10   50   100   300   500   1,000   5,000   15,000   25,000

Circle the number of people you are currently leading.

2   5   10   50   100   300   500   1,000   5,000   15,000   25,000

What is the gap between your potential and reality?

_____

How many times have you grown beyond your current number?

_____

If you are stuck at a number, ask yourself, "What is it going to take to get to the next level?"

_____

If you did not circle 25,000, then you must commit to changing and growing as a leader.

_____

What do you have to change to get better?

_____

Every person on your leadership team has to move up the scale on their leadership abilities. If you don't move up and they don't move up, you are never going to get to your goal no matter how hard you work, pray, and believe. If there is no real deep-seated improvement in the team, then the organizational potential is limited by the team that is around the leader. This brings us to the next axiom, which is the Law of the Lid.

2. The Law of the Lid

This concept came from John Maxwell and I have taught, adapted, and shaped it for years into the following insights. When you get this law inside you, it will be a driving force. Leadership ability is the lid that determines a person's level of impact, influence, and income. The lower an individual's ability to lead, the lower the lid on his or her potential.

LQ Solution: In order to DOUBLE your influence, impact, and income, you must TRIPLE your learning.

The preceding graph illustrates this point of doubling and tripling. Both represent an average person who has a desire to make a difference, influence others, and increase his or her income. The first graph illustrates a very hard-working or productive person without leadership skills. This person has a measure of success, but doesn't have good leadership skills. However, the person has a leadership position. If this person does not continue to grow personally in leadership knowledge, his or her effectiveness and potential for impact, influence, and income are going to be very limited.

Now look at the other graph titled "Impact *with* Leadership." This graph illustrates a person with the exact same abilities and work ethic but with added leadership skills for influencing others. This person has started to daily develop leadership skills. His leadership skill level has risen from two to six. This person is not working harder. However, his success, influence, impact, and income have increased by 600 percent. This person's ability to increase leadership skills completely changes the landscape of that person's potential.

When I look back to that little church out in the middle of nowhere, I was the guy at two on this scale. I worked hard over the years to increase my leadership skills, and now I am at six. I see the level of impact I made back then compared to now, and I know it is all because I've learned that success is not built in a day. Success is built over time through a process. It is not the big event we've attended; it is what we do daily that makes the difference.

LQ Solution: Success is built over time through a process. It is what we do daily that makes the difference.

The Law of the Lid says, "Leaders attract other leaders who are equal to or below them, but will rarely attract leaders with skills above them." It's not necessarily your spirituality that determines how much of a difference you make in the earth. It is your ability to grow and build your leadership skills, equip and reproduce leaders, and thereby leave a legacy. I have met some of the most spiritual people in the world in my travels in hundreds of churches, but sadly most of them are broke, busted, and disgusted. They are making no impact in the earth.

When my first church was stuck at approximately 150 people, I realized that in order to grow further I had to improve my LQ. I had to work hard on transitioning from a minister mind-set to a leader mind-set. I had to keep raising the bar on my leadership lid. I discovered that as I started to work on my LQ, my church started growing. The interesting thing is both our quality and quantity increased. We started to attract people from all strata of culture—both down-and-outers as well as up-and-outers, wealthy and poor, blue collars and professionals. The mayor of a nearby city came, then the city attorney, and next the owner of the newspaper of the region started attending our church. I noticed that the more I worked on and taught leadership, the more leaders came to our church. We became a magnet in our region for other Christian leaders. That was what really helped us make a greater impact in our small community.

Self-Evaluation

Work through the Rate Yourself box on the following page. Then proceed with your study of this chapter.

Rate Yourself

Where would you rate yourself as a leader on a scale from 1 to 10 on the chart? Before you do that, here are some parameters to help you more accurately determine where you are. Judge yourself by how many people are following you. Somebody once said, "If you think you are a leader and you are moving forward but nobody is following you, then you are just out for a walk."

How many people are following you?_____

To be rated as a ten would mean you have read one hundred books on leadership, and you have over 150 people following you and looking to you for leadership.

To be rated as a five you have a group of 50-150 people following you and you have read at least ten books on leadership.

One would be you telling me this is the first time you have heard any of this stuff. You understand it and realize you are just starting out on this journey. Nobody is really following you at this point. You know you have not risen above an average person.

| 1 | 2 | 3 | 4 | 5 | 6 | 7 | 8 | 9 | 10 |

When I first heard this, I rated myself at a three. And the Law of the Lid says if the leader is a three like I was at 150 people in my church, I will only attract people who are two, one, or zero to my ministry. So when I was a three, if the mayor was a seven, he would not want to come to my church. He might come and visit one time, but he wouldn't want to come back even though he didn't really know why. Because he was a seven, he looked at things from a totally different perspective from a three or a two.

A seven would say this pastor who is only a three as a leader doesn't even have a vision for the church. Are we just coming here to sing worship choruses? What is this guy doing? Where is he going? It isn't clear, so the seven doesn't come back.

This law is rarely if ever violated, even though there are a few times when somebody who is a high-level leader will stay under a lower-level leader, usually because they have searched hard to find a church to attend and settled with a leader who has skills below them. But if the pastor stays at three and a seven stays, there is eventually going to be a conflict. If the seven stays long enough, he is going to be the greater influencer and may take over.

If the youth pastor, administrator, children's pastor, or the worship leader is rated at three, the whole ministry is stuck there. Longevity does not mean maturity. Just because they have been in a position for a long time does not mean that they are mature. If the worship leader has been there forever but never gets better leadership skills, that part of that ministry will be stuck, which affects the rest of the ministries. The corporate leadership team shapes whether we have great organizational success or not. So if one person on the team refuses to grow, it stops all from growing.

A football team can have a world-class quarterback, but if there is a lineman on the team who doesn't train and work out over the summer break, he gets fat and slow. No matter how great the quarterback is, the lineman will continually let the defensive guy get by him and tackle the quarterback before he can even throw the ball. The quarterback is stopped because a person on the team hasn't grown. It is the same thing in every organization. Every person who holds a leadership position has to be passionate about growing as a leader.

LQ Coaching Questions

1. What would you do with this lineman if you were his coach?

   _____

2. Do you have any fat, slow linemen on your team?

   _____

3. What should you do about them?_____

   _____

4. Have you provided a "training camp" to help them get into leadership shape?

   _____

I suggest you set a personal goal to increase your leadership skills two points every year. So in one year, you will have increased your leadership skills by reading more books, listening to more CDs, and applying what you have learned. Focus your time and energies on developing both your spirituality and your leadership skills. Then by this time next year, you can come back to this page and write down that you are now a five.

If you do this and grow from a three to a five, you will begin to attract those who are four, three, two, and one, and you will have doubled your leadership capacity. The secret is to then set your goal to grow another two points the following year. When you have become a seven, you will now attract all those who are six and below. At this point you have tripled your potential.

A church will not grow beyond its leadership capacity and its ability to care for people. We have heard this concept in our personal lives as, "The Lord won't give you any more than you can handle" (see 1 Corinthians 10:13). During the next year, you can continue to grow if you inspire all of the leaders around you to get hungry and increase their LQ and grow themselves to their maximum potential.

Increase Your Lid

First, make a determination that you are going to learn more this year than you ever have before. Leaders are readers. Even if you haven't caught a lot because you haven't had good examples, you can do as I did. You can teach yourself by focusing your energies on the materials that will improve your ability to lead. You have got to zoom in on leadership; in the mornings, read the Bible to develop yourself spiritually. At night, turn off the television and read a book on leadership. Start somewhere, and do it every day of your life. That is the quickest way to start lifting your lid.

Second, experience what you have learned. Dare to move beyond yourself and step out of yourself—that is what leadership is really all about. Martin Luther King Jr. said, "It is easy to be a leader because when it is time to do something, the majority of the people will take a step back." We need leaders who will take a step up. Leadership means being out in front and willing to take responsibility for what needs to happen in your organization. Learning skills without the ability to put them to use is useless.

3. The Law of Quality

We are living in a day when we make two major mistakes as leaders: Mistake 1, we tend to focus on faster and bigger. And

Mistake 2, we have gone after the down-and-outers, but forgotten the up-and-outers.

Let's look more closely at Mistake 1. We want everything faster and bigger, but we need to realize faster and bigger does not always mean *better*. As a matter of fact, sometimes we sacrifice excellence for speed and size. Instead of focusing on bigger, focus on getting better! When you get better, you will automatically get bigger.

LQ Solution: Small, daily improvements over time lead to phenomenal results.

When I was pastoring that little church, I was so fortunate to be able to go once a month to visit with a pastor who was overseeing a much larger church. He gave me an hour of his time and shared his leadership secrets with me. I wanted to understand what he did to grow his church. One of the very first things he did was tell me to write down the name of every department of ministry in the church. Then he told me to draw the layout of our building—inside and outside. He wanted to know about everything from our sound system to the yard surrounding the church. He told me to list all of my current resources. Then he told me to use a scale of 1 to 10 and rate everything—the paint, the music ministry, the sound board, children's church, everything. I did just that.

Then he introduced me to a very important law, the Law of Quality. He told me to take that scale and every year go back over the list and look at every area. "Then ask yourself," he said, "How can I improve this by at least two points in the next year? How can I make everything a little bit better?" He told me if I would do that every year, he guaranteed our entire ministry would grow.

I am going to challenge you to do the very same thing—because I know it works. Lay out everything, then rate it and ask yourself, "How can we do it just a little bit better? What can we do to improve things two points in the next year?" These questions apply not only to the physical parts of your church, but the people parts as well. Your human resources are your greatest assets. When things start getting better within your team and you raise the quality of each member of your team, the quality of your team goes up. *You have to see an improvement in quality before you will ever see a rise in quantity.* Small improvements over time produce incredible results.

LQ Solution: Too many leaders fool themselves into thinking they have fulfilled their potential and that their organizations are running as effectively and efficiently as possible.

I totally agree with Marshall Goldsmith, popular CEO coach for many Fortune 500 companies, who made this observation, "Successful people are incredibly delusional about their achievements. Over 95 percent of members in most successful groups believe that they perform in the top half of their group. While this is statistically ridiculous, it is psychologically real."

Here are two simple but profound coaching questions to help you put your leadership skills and abilities into proper perspective:

1. Can you leave?

When I am coaching business leaders, I start by giving them my definition of a business: A commercial enterprise that produces a profit without me. The last phrase is profound— without me. Then I ask, "If you left your business for one month, what would happen to your organization?" Most small business owners admit it would fall apart, which shows lack of leadership. They have spent all kinds of time working "in" their business versus working "on" the business. The same principle applies to churches and nonprofit organizations. If you took a one-month sabbatical, what would happen to your church? Sadly, most leaders admit things would fall apart.

2. Are you lonely?

Sometimes I will open my leadership conference by asking, "How many of you know that when you are a leader, it is lonely at the top?" Almost everybody raises their hand. Actually, if you feel lonely at the top, you are doing something wrong!

LQ Solution: Inviting feedback is an essential skill to increase your leadership quotient.

Successful people have two problems with dealing with feedback. 1) They don't want to really hear it. 2) Their followers don't want to give it to them. We naturally accept feedback that is consistent with our self-image and reject feedback that is inconsistent. The challenge: most people's self-image is all messed up.

The Hamburger Tool is the proof that leadership is a skill. Very few CEOs know this skill—but now you are going to learn all about it.

Scripture exhorts us to be imitators of God, and God is into excellence. Excellence is the continual pursuit of improvement. We need to continually improve ourselves. All of us think we are doing our best at what we are doing. Nobody wants to think he or she has a horrible life or career. But our best can always get a little better. Right?

Based on my many years of experience, in order to get better, everyone needs a coach. You need somebody who is outside of your picture frame to give you objective insight. When you are in the picture, you can't accurately see the full picture. We all need feedback from an outside source—a coach or mentor—to get better perspective. Ken Blanchard said, "Feedback is the breakfast of champions." I agree.

Your leadership team needs coaching to make things better. Unfortunately, church members are often insecure. We want things to get better, but if we challenge people to change in order to improve, their insecurity registers feedback as criticism. Because most people are insecure, instead of giving feedback, we tend to hide it under the rug. We accept mediocrity because we don't want people to feel badly. So eventually, everything we do is at a lower standard than the world instead of having a higher standard. To improve, we must learn to use tools to help people feel good about receiving feedback. Hence, the Law of the Hamburger becomes necessary.

For example, an usher needs some feedback: *buns* are praise, the *meat* is the feedback. The bun on the top is praise. Take the time to make the person feel good about their current performance. Praise them for effort. Tell the usher something positive about the way he or she is doing their ministry such as, "You have a great smile," or "What a positive attitude you have." Sincerely build up the person and make him or her feel important.

But if all you do is praise, you are not motivating the person to improve. You must go through the entire hamburger, the bun and now the meat. The meat is the feedback, but your delivery is very important. Don't go into the meeting thinking confrontation—rather think clarification. Do not make it sound like judgment or criticism. Tell the usher you are sure he wants to be the best usher the church has ever seen, so you would like to offer some positive suggestions to improve his job and bring it up to a spirit of excellence that you know he wants to achieve. Offer your feedback as a positive not a negative. Feedback starts with the "what" and then goes to the "why." It is not the "what," it is the "why" that causes an action.

Explain why this change in his approach to ushering needs to be done. Offer suggestions on how to do it and possibly point out that he skipped a step or exemplifies the wrong impression. For example, if he forgot to wear his name badge for three Sundays in a row, point out how important it is that members of the congregation and visitors can identify him as an usher. Impress how important he is because he welcomes both current and new attendees.

The bottom bun is more praise in the form of encouraging him to strive for this new level of excellence; stressing his importance in the organization. Let him know of your appreciation for his faithful service, and tell him you look forward to seeing him with his name badge on next Sunday.

When people receive the right feedback, you gain better staff and ministry volunteers—and future leaders. If this isn't the case, you may discover that some people need to be moved within the church body to positions that are better suited to their skills, personalities, or talents.

Mistake 2 – We have gone after the down-and-outers, but have forgotten the up-and-outers.

I was sharing this mistake we had made at a church one day, and the pastor said to me, "Well, it just seems that God has called this church to reach the down-and-outers. God has called this church to go after the people nobody else cares about. Seems like poor people are attracted to this place. Every Monday for the past fifteen years, we have prayed for all the poor people in our city."

As he concluded his statement, I asked, "So on Tuesday do you pray for the rich people in the city?" He was obviously surprised by my question as he responded, "Why, no." Then I probed a little further, "Do you ever pray for the influential and rich people in your city? Do you pray for governmental leaders? What about people who sit on the school board? What about those who control the media in your area? What about the successful business owners?" Each question he responded by shaking his head, "No."

Then I said, "What you are telling me is that you've attracted exactly what you have prayed for...only poor, noninfluential people." The pastor realized his mistake and started praying for both classes of people, and his church started attracting people from both walks of life.

How long does it take to move Harry the Hobo into leadership positions versus moving the mayor of your city into leadership? We have already established that your ability to succeed is based on your ability to train up leaders; the faster the better. We target Harry the Hobo and wonder why we don't have any leaders. God has been giving the church exactly what we have been praying and asking for. It is important to realize we need both quantity and quality to experience true church health and growth to effectively transform our culture.

LQ Solution: When you increase your quality, your quantity will automatically increase.

Down-and-Outers & Up-and-Outers

We have failed to attract quality people to our churches because our target has been to reach the poor and suffering. Our target should also include influencing the up-and-outers. How are we going to disciple nations if we don't reach highly influential people?

- Are the down-and-outers or the up-and-outers easier to move into leadership quickly?

- Which one of these groups has more influence in your city, region, and nation?

Many churches have a poverty mentality; we think only the poor want God. Out of our insecurities we have only gone after the poor because it strokes our egos. It makes us feel good. We are up here and they are down there and that makes us feel good. To go after those who are at a higher level than we are challenges our confidence levels.

During one of my leadership trainings, a person blurted out from the crowd, "The rich don't want anything to do with God!" I then kindly asked the person, "How do you know that? Who told you that? How many millionaires did you witness to last week?"

Bonnie and I are blessed to live in an upper echelon, gated community, and I found out that there are more police calls for domestic violence in our community than elsewhere. Three houses down the street from our home, the most prominent doctor in our area killed his wife. We may think wealthy people don't want God, but they do. The up-and-outers have material and financial success, but many don't have God.

To be poor means to be without. It does not necessarily mean "without money." It may mean "without God, without values, without hope, without friends, or without self-confidence." If a person is without God, they are just as poor as Harry the Hobo; yet we have totally left that group of people out of our target audience. This is a big mistake. We must change our mind-set and refocus our evangelistic strategy. If we are going to change the culture of our region, we have to get to where we are comfortable inviting the mayor of our city to our church services. The up-and-outers are hungry.

I have a coaching business, and most people who come for my training are Christians. The first thing they try to do after the training is to get Christians in the church as clients to coach. I tell them not to go after Christians, go after sinners. I have two reasons for telling them that:

1. Christians are usually cheap and don't have extra money. Sinners invest in coaching because they don't have a pastor or attend church.

2. We want to convert the sinner and make him or her a saint. So use your coaching business to reach sinners.

Our coaching organization wins more people to Christ than most churches do in a year. I teach our coaches to target the up-and-outers. When my coaches land an up-and-outer client, they discover these people are open to spiritual matters. It is exactly opposite of what most people think.

Here is the new way of thinking I am introducing to you: *It is not either-or, it can be both.* Put just as much effort, money, and time in going after the up-and-outers in our countries and cities as we do the down-and-outers. When you start winning the up-and-outers, bring them into your church and give them a solid discipleship program. I found that a year later, you can move them right into leadership because they already have the basic leadership abilities to achieve their current status. When we target the down-and-outers, it could take ten or twenty years to develop an effective leadership team in your organization. Your whole team will move forward, but very, very slowly.

When you have a high *quality* ministry, you will attract a higher *quantity* of people. Make a commitment to continually better your best. Strive to become the best you can be, and stir up a passion in your heart that says, "I was destined to lead, and I am going to develop my leadership skills and bring them to an all-time high."

Now that we have debunked the myths and laid a foundation with the "Three Laws of Leadership" for your leadership quotient, let's look at the most important asset to increasing your Leadership Quotient—assurance.

Unleash Your LQ

- How have your rated yourself as a leader? What goal have you set for yourself to help you grow? What will you do to accomplish your goal?

- Start a journey. Write down stories about the times you have used the Law of the Hamburger and detail how that law has impacted your effectiveness as a leader.

- What is your leadership potential?

- How many people can you lead right now?

- What can your organization handle at this stage of the game?

- What do you think is the threshold of what your team can handle?

- List the community leaders in your region. Start praying for them by name. If you do not know specifically how to pray for them, pray the Lord's Prayer over their lives, work, and families.

- What community actions can you take to serve your community, being light and salt where you live? Government? Business associates? Education? Entertainment? Media?

Assurance is freedom from doubt; belief in yourself and your abilities. In times of economic crisis, CONFIDENCE is the flickering candle that a leader cannot allow to be extinguished. As a leader, you must keep the horizon of the future of your organization full of promise.
–Dr. Keith Johnson

Humility is a virtue: Timidity is a disease!
–Jim Rohn

When we are truly confident and secure, the opinions of others cannot control us.
–Joyce Meyers

I discovered that the thinking of a leader is what separates him or her from the followers. I found that true leaders are distinguished by a unique mental attitude that emanates from an internalized discovery of self, which creates a strong, positive, and confident self-concept and self-worth.
–Myles Munroe

Perhaps the greatest single gift she gave me was self-confidence. It's what I've looked for and tried to build in every executive who has ever worked for me. Confidence gives you courage and extends your reach. It lets you take greater risk and achieve far more than you ever thought possible. Building self-confidence in others is a huge part of leadership. It comes from providing opportunities and challenges for people to do things they never imagined they could do— rewarding them after each success in every way possible.
– Jack Welch, Former CEO of General Electric

CHAPTER SIX

ASSURANCE

Confident Leaders Produce Committed Followers

What is the number one missing ingredient in church leadership today? Consider this scenario: Two high school graduates attend the same Bible college excited about the call of God to pastor a thriving church some day. Both took the same classes, achieved excellent grades, became excellent speakers, and had a solid understanding about biblical truth. Both graduated and pastored churches in thriving suburban areas.

Although both of these pastors have the same background, talent, education, and ministry opportunities, one pastor built a church where thousands of excited churchgoers gather every Sunday morning. Sadly, the other pastor has struggled for fourteen years with less than one hundred church members.

What is the major difference between the two pastors? Does God love one more than the other? Does one pray harder? Is one in a better location? Does the enemy fight one more than the other? The answer is, "NO!"

What is the difference? The Confidence Factor.

For the past sixteen years I have studied leaders, leadership, and church growth and have ministered in hundreds of churches. I have personally coached hundreds of pastors, and over the years have discovered the major difference is confidence!

If there is one quality you could have that would make you successful in motivating people or convincing people to follow your lead, that trait would be CONFIDENCE. –Dr. John Maxwell

Ministries are suffering from the lack of leadership confidence. The Barna Research Group and Fuller seminary released these statistics revealing the need for pastors to boost their confidence:

- 70 percent of pastors said their self-image is lower now than when they entered into the ministry.

- 90 percent of pastors reported that they felt inadequate for the tasks before them.

- 95 percent of pastors say they don't have the leadership gifts to perform in the way that their congregations expect them to perform.

- 75 percent of pastors responded anonymously that they are intimidated by the lay leaders or staff.

- 65 percent of pastors said that they have seriously considered quitting the ministry within the last two months.

What can we learn from these statistics?

We can conclude that 75-95 percent of pastoral leaders in America struggle with confidence.

Do you identify with any of these statistics? If so, this chapter will help.

LQ: Rarely will the confidence levels of a follower be higher than the leaders who lead them.

If the leaders in our pulpits are struggling with low-confidence issues, poor self-image, low self-esteem, and feelings of failure, what kind of confidence levels will there be in the people sitting in our churches every Sunday?

Your personal insecurities create an invisible "glass lid" that keeps you, your congregation, and your church from growing to maximum capacity and potential. This chapter takes you on a journey to create a more confident you. When you increase your personal confidence, you will unleash your true potential and maximize your performance. Those invisible barriers will be destroyed, launching you and your ministry to the next level—and beyond!

An army of sheep led by a lion will always defeat an army of lions lead by a sheep. Many leaders have associated with sheep so much that they try to lead like a sheep when they are to lead like a lion.

From Senior Pastor to Baggage Carrier

A few years ago, in a private leadership coaching session, I lovingly told a pastor about his insecurities and that he needed to work on building his confidence so his ministry would grow. The pastor dismissed my advice and insisted that his "personal level of confidence had nothing to do with growing his church." Unfortunately, over the next few years, his church membership declined, along with his personal confidence. Now he works as a baggage carrier at a Florida airport. What a tragedy! Don't let this happen to you.

My Own Lack of Confidence

Just ten years ago I was so frustrated with my own ministry that I wanted to quit and get a secular job! I went through the whole "blame game" routine. I blamed my wife, my church members, my staff, the geographical location, the devil, and even God for the lack of growth and success in my ministry. Thankfully my life and ministry changed the day I discovered what the real problem was—I lacked confidence!

The greatest asset of a leader is confidence. The greatest liability of a leader is insecurity. –Dr. John Maxwell

The number one cry I hear from many senior pastors is, "Nobody is committed anymore!" Confidence is contagious. People do not commit to anything unless they experience the feeling of confidence. When a leader is full of FUD (Fear, Uncertainty, Doubt), followers pick it up. When a leader lacks confidence, followers lack the confidence needed to take action to make the commitment to help you build your God-given dream.

LQ Solution: When a leader exudes confidence, followers reward you with commitment.

When you study the word "faith" in the Bible, you find three key words associated with that word:

- Belief

- Action

- Confidence

Let's look at each word in more detail:

Key Word 1: BELIEF

Faith starts when you know God's will and truth. The foundation of faith in anything starts with what you know and believe. The church today is full of people who know and believe a lot of Bible doctrine; yet it is possible to believe something but not actually practice or live what you believe. Your actions must be rooted in the truth of Scripture.

Key Word 2: ACTION

Faith without corresponding actions cannot be called faith. Faith without works is worse than no faith at all. Verbal and mental faith is insufficient. Faith must inspire action. The apostle James teaches us that it is impossible to have faith without corresponding actions (see James 1:22-25; 2:14-20,24-26).

This is where the problem lies in the modern-day church. Many Christians believe a lot of different things. However, most confessing Christians do not actually follow through with what they believe. For instance:

- The majority of Christians believe they should tithe, but only 5 to 12 percent actually tithe on a regular basis.

- Everyone believes we should be evangelizing the lost for Jesus Christ. Sadly, only 2 percent of modern churchgoers have ever won another person to Christ.

- We believe we should read the Bible. Fewer people are reading the Bible these days; only one-third do so in a typical week.

- Most Christians believe they are called to do something wonderful with their lives. However, most people in our churches today are broke, busted, and disgusted.

- Most Christians believe we should take care of our bodies—God's temple. However, most believers are overweight, don't exercise, and have some sort of health problem.

- We believe that a senior pastor should lead the church by God's vision. Less than one out of every ten senior pastors can articulate what they believe is God's vision for the church they are leading.

Hopefully you can see the gap. The gap between what Christians "believe" and what they actually "do."

What is keeping us from actually doing what we claim we believe?

The answer is found in the third key word in faith, *confidence.*

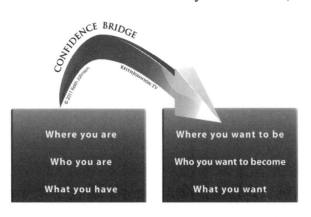

Key Word 3: CONFIDENCE

*"So do not throw away your **confidence**; it will be richly rewarded"* (Hebrews 10:35, emphasis added). Confidence bridges the gap between what you believe and what you actually do. When confidence is taken out of the faith equation, you have a group of people who are constantly learning a new truth but never experiencing the joy of applying it in their lives. Therefore, they never end up reaping the rewards and benefits of the promises found in the Word of God.

Have you been caught in the vicious cycle of going to church, hearing another sermon or teaching, learning another truth, being inspired in the moment, and then going home to live a life that does not line up with what you have learned? Christians caught in this cycle of "sit, soak, and sour" become disappointed in themselves and others as leaders. They criticize leadership and become cynical, often dropping out of church and the active pursuit of God. Why? Because the more you learn about what you should be doing, the more you begin to realize that there is a gap between where you really are and where you should be.

Everything we receive in life is by faith—what we believe and confidence to take our belief and turn it into a corresponding action. The apostle Paul was undoubtedly a great achiever. He was responsible for taking the gospel to Rome and ultimately around the word. He was also an accomplished author who wrote almost two-thirds of the New Testament. This legendary achiever gave you the key to unleashing the lion within and becoming the champion God called you to be:

> *Do you not know that in a race all the runners run, but only one gets the prize? Run in such a way as to get the prize. ...Therefore I do not run like a man running aimlessly; I do not fight like a man beating the air (1 Corinthians 9:24-26).*

You were born to win. The key to attaining the prize and winning in life is to overcome your insecurities so you can function and operate on a daily basis in supreme confidence. The majority of people in the world today are underachievers. Why? Because many spend most of their lives shadowboxing themselves. Until you learn to conquer yourself, you will continue to "beat the air"—fighting through life, but not achieving any real progress. Have you ever felt like you take three steps forward only to take five steps backward? Are you tired of living life in cycles of defeat and failure?

Apostle Paul learned not to run through life with insecurity. Champions exude confidence. Paul was no longer fighting the shadow of himself, as evidenced by his writing in 1 Corinthians 9:24-26. You, too, can learn to live without insecurity.

I am not only getting older in life, I am personally maturing and realizing that the greatest enemy to my LQ is me! I have done more personal harm to myself than any person, any church, or any devil. Yes, the greatest devil I fight is the one I look at in the mirror in the morning. When I learn to beat myself, then and only then, am I ready for the real enemy.

LQ Solution: You must conquer yourself before you qualify to enter into the winner's circle.

Unleash the Lion Within

Why is the lion considered the king of the jungle? Because he's the biggest, fastest, most handsome, hardest working animal in the jungle? No! So why is he the king, the animal others respect? Because he's the most confident! I have discovered that this truth in the jungle is also true in the church, financial, business, and cultural jungles in which we live.

...the righteous are bold as a lion (Proverbs 28:1).

It is time for you to awaken the lion in you! There is a lion living inside you—and that lion will make you bold and confident. Jesus is called the Lion of the tribe of Judah (see Revelation 5:5-6). Within you has been birthed the new creation nature of Christ whom you are becoming more like moment by moment. Consider God's nature that has been imparted to you through Christ:

> *Listen! Listen to the roar of his voice, to the rumbling that comes from his mouth. He unleashes his lightning beneath the whole heaven and sends it to the ends of the earth. After that comes the sound of his roar; he thunders with his majestic voice. When his voice resounds, he holds nothing back. God's voice thunders in marvelous ways; he does great things beyond our understanding (Job 37:2-5).*

When will you silence your insecure murmurings and allow His roar to sound through you?

**LQ Solution: Confidence in the Lord will
always take you to the top.**

When God wants to use somebody in the earth, He looks for a confident man or woman. Think about it, out of the twelve disciples, who did Jesus chose to use when He needed something done? John loved Jesus more than all the disciples, but John was not chosen for divine leadership opportunities (see John 13:23; 19:25-27; 20:2; 21:20). Jesus picked Peter. Why? *Peter was the most confident disciple.*

Peter: A Lion of a Leader

Peter was a man of action. Insecure leaders are passive, which produces poverty. Confident leaders are persistent and produce prosperity. Peter was Jesus' confident giant, even though Peter had great trials and failures. Confidence always takes you back to the top, even when you are down and out.

Peter's confidence revealed:

1. Peter walked on water (see Matthew 14:28-31).

2. He was the first disciple to declare that Jesus was the Christ (see Matthew 16:16).

3. Even after being rebuked by Jesus, Peter did not take offense but continued on with Him (see Matthew 16:23).

4. Peter was willing to fight for Jesus (see John 18:10).

5. He stayed with Jesus the longest (see Matthew 26:56,58).

6. Peter bounced back from failure (see John 21:15).

7. He was the first disciple to enter into the empty tomb of Jesus (see John 20:5-6).

8. Peter preached the first Gospel message after Pentecost (see Acts 2:14-24).

9. He brought the Gospel to the Gentiles (see Acts 10).

10. Peter died for the Lord *(Foxe's Book of Martyrs).*

I am often asked, "How do I know when I have become a really confident person?"

My answer, "You will know you have become an extremely confident person when other people start calling you cocky."

Insecure people always view and judge your confidence as arrogance. Remember, they did it to David when he was confident he could kill Goliath. When people call you arrogant, stay confident anyway! What's the difference between arrogance and confidence?

Arrogance:

- Focuses the spotlight on self; confidence focuses on God.

- Uses people and loves things; confidence uses things and loves people.

- Wants glory; confidence gives glory and honor to God and others.

- Is rooted in pride; confidence is rooted in what God's Word says about you.

Make it a priority to become a confident giant in the earth so God will chose you when He looks for somebody to do something extraordinary. Leading others requires confidence. Why? *Knowing* the right decision is the easy part of leadership. *Making* the right decision is the hard part of leadership. Confidence prevents the leader from having three negative feelings:

1. Fear of people

2. Dislike for people

3. Contempt for people

If you are afraid of people, you cannot and will not handle them with compassion. If you dislike people, you cannot lead them into their destinies. If you look down on people, they will not respect you.

Confident leaders take responsibility when things go wrong. However, when everything goes well, they don't take the credit. They praise the team and give the team the credit. The modern American church has lost its influence in shaping the culture of the nation, and it is time we get it back! Instead of acting like fearful mice, it's time for the lions to roar.

Ready to increase your LQ? Then walk in the confidence imparted to you by Christ, the Lion of Judah!

Unleash Your LQ

- Identify your insecurities. Find a trusted Christian friend, coach, leader, trainer, or mentor. Ask him or her to help you move from insecurity in yourself to confidence in God.

- Read my books, *The Confidence Solution* and *Confidence at Work*.

- What fears, uncertainties, and doubts need to die inside you? What qualities of confidence need to emerge from Christ's lion nature in you?

- Do you allow the three Ns to destroy your confidence? Nickels, Numbers, and the Nodes?

The single biggest way to impact an organization is to focus on leadership development. There is almost no limit to the potential of an organization that recruits good people, raises them up as leaders and continually develops them.

–John C. Maxwell

The 21 Irrefutable Laws of Teamwork

We have all heard it said, "If it's going to be, it's up to me." Although this is a very strong statement and many entrepreneurs believe it up to this point, it carries also some negative aspects with it as well. If I believe that the only way things are going to happen in this life is that I must do it, I have violated one of my major principles in life— TEAMWORK. There is no "I" in team. Team building and team actions are what really make the difference.

–Ed Mercer

The Power of Leadership

The sight of achievement is the greatest gift a human being could offer others.

–Ayn Rand

Libertarian Viewpoint

CHAPTER SEVEN

ACHIEVEMENT

Leaders Have a Stop Doing List

True achievement is the ability to perform, carry out, and accomplish, especially something difficult. Busyness involves expended time and energy but not necessarily productivity. Leadership and management expert Peter Drucker said, "We spend a lot of time teaching leaders what to do. We don't spend enough time teaching leaders what to stop. Half the leaders I have met don't need to learn what to do. They need to learn what to stop."

Instead of a "to do list," most pastors and leaders need a "not to do list."

Every Saturday night of the year, I have dedicated myself to conducting a church leaders' seminar. No matter where I am in the world, I always ask the group, "What is the number one barrier to church growth?" The answers I receive vary greatly—from better music, lack of evangelism, being nicer to visitors, to needing a new building. The list goes on and on. In all the years of helping people develop their LQ, I have never had a crowd identify the real problem—the real barrier to church growth.

In my experience, the number one barrier to church growth is the hyperbusyness of the senior pastor. Just because you are busy does not mean you are making progress or reaping success. Your busyness may be keeping you from developing and training others to be the leaders they are called to be in the Kingdom.

The life and ministry of Moses changed the day Jethro gave Moses a word of wisdom saying, "Moses, you are doing too much! You need a stop doing list! Stop working harder and start working smarter by training others to do what you are doing. If you continue at this pace, you are going to burn out!" (Exodus 18:13-27, my paraphrase). Moses needed to learn the "work" of leadership delegation.

Moses decided to change two things that positively transformed his life and ministry:

1. His way of thinking, and most importantly

2. His way of working

It is both natural and necessary for a pastor or Christian leader in any sphere of influence to be a leader and set the pace in the church. It is often necessary to do almost everything yourself because you don't have others to help you. But what was natural and necessary in the beginning, over a period of time, limits your effectiveness. Some pastors and small business owners are so busy that they do everything themselves without raising up leaders around them. Every leader has two jobs—doing the work of a leader and training a leader to take his or her place. Failure to raise up leaders and delegate responsibilities results in burnout.

I have taught these leadership solutions to friends who now pastor churches with several thousand members:

LQ Solution 1—The less you do, the more you accomplish.

LQ Solution 2—The less you do yourself, the more you enable others to accomplish.[1]

LQ Solution 3— The less you speak, the more authority and influence you have when you do speak.

The Ultimate Question

Is your time consumed with endless counseling sessions, putting out church "fires," hospital visitations, telephone interruptions, and other such tasks of the ministry?

Many pastors and church leaders were taught in college that it was a leader's responsibility, in business or the church, to do things right. And that if we wanted something done right, we should do it ourselves. Consequently, many leaders and pastors today do not spend quality time developing their leadership and communication skills.

The majority of your time should be spent doing only two things: 1) Preparing great (not good) messages every time you speak; 2) Mentoring your leadership team. Outside these two things, other tasks should be on your not to do list. Senior pastors are called to "PREACH THE GOSPEL!" Therefore, you are called to be a world class communicator!

You are *not:*

- a counselor for people's marital problems,

- a fighting family's referee,

- a judge to decide who is at fault,

- a bank to lend people money,

- an attorney to provide legal advice,

- a nurse to take care of wounds,

- a mechanic to fix their cars,

- a construction worker to repair their homes,

- a moving company to help people relocate.

While your ministry may include doing some of these tasks and equipping others to do them, your primary calling is communication. Your ability to effectively communicate as a leader is an essential skill in motivating and moving the masses. I am amazed how many pastors, politicians, educators, and business leaders do not study the principles of communication. The average family today, by television, is exposed to as many as five hours a day of world-class communicators. They have the advantage of teleprompters and professional writers who write their scripts. They are able to get their point across in two-minute sound bites on the news and thirty seconds in a commercial.

LQ Solution – Confusion, problems, and hours of wasted time are the reward of those who do not take communications seriously.

No one can be a successful leader who does not endeavor to communicate effectively. If you are going to influence people and draw people to helping you fulfill your dream, you cannot be a mediocre communicator. You are called to be an outstanding world-class communicator. In order for you to achieve this goal, you must stand out. The difference between the amateur and professional communicators is one key principle—they spend more time in preparation!

Due to the hyperbusyness of the senior pastor, many fall into the trap of just "winging" their messages. After all, if you are not prepared, you can always rely on your ministry gift to pull you through, right? Wrong.

When you get into a cycle of "winging" your sermons, you make two critical mistakes:

1. Your messages are way too long. Eighty-five percent of megachurch pastors speak less than thirty minutes. Yet most sermons I hear can be made into a four-week series. The shorter the message, the more preparation required. I need hardly any preparation time to speak for a two-hour seminar. However, when FOX News gave me a two-minute interview about my book, it took me two weeks to prepare just the right words. Hint: for great impact, make just one powerful point for the entire message.

2. You become out of touch with the real needs of the people. When you are not effectively communicating, you speak:

- From the head and not your heart.

- About yesterday and not today.

- From what you have learned and not what you are learning.

- From what you have done and not what you are doing.

- Words that entertain people, but fail to change lives!

The Solution

The first promise I make to pastors about my leadership coaching program: "I am going to help you take plates off your desk. When I am finished, you will feel guilty about not being so busy. However, you will actually have time to prepare great messages and spend quality time with your wife, children, and friends."

How can you take your church or business to the next level? Invest your time developing and training your leadership team. Statistics show for each person you develop and train in the church for leadership, you will enable your church to grow by twenty to one hundred members or more. Your church cannot grow beyond the width and depth of your leadership structure because you cannot grow beyond your ability to serve and care for the people.

*Will this be the year you finally get serious
about Leadership Training?*

**LQ Solution: The size of the structure determines
the size of the organization.**

Great churches and organizations are built on strong leaders and great structure. Many organizations have highly-gifted leaders, but do not have the necessary leadership structure in place to facilitate significant growth. Membership at most churches in America is at a plateau or declining because they simply cannot handle more growth. Remember, the Scriptures teach us that the Lord will not give us more than we can handle. Maybe your organization or ministry is not growing because your current leadership structure cannot handle it.

Think about this...how much skeletal structure is needed for an amoeba (the smallest living organism)? None! It actually has no skeletal system. How big is the skeletal structure of an elephant? Huge! How big do you want your organization to grow? Do you want amoeba, mouse, dog, horse, or elephant size? In order to increase the size of your church, you must first improve the size of your structure.

An Important Church Growth Key

While much I will now say focuses on pastors, the same principles also apply in business. Statistics show for each person you develop and train in the church for leadership, you will enable your church to grow significantly. Your church cannot grow beyond the width and depth of your leadership structure because you cannot grow beyond your ability to serve and care for the people. According to Ephesians 4:11-16, your responsibility as a leader is threefold:

1. **DISCOVER.** You are to help people discover their future in Christ, gifts, and talents so they can be used for the work of the ministry.

2. **DEVELOP.** After you discover the people's gifts, you can develop their gifts with practical training information and hands-on instruction.

3. **DEPLOY.** When they have been thoroughly trained, you must release them to start doing the work of the ministry.

There are only two ways to grow a ministry:

1. **Grow the senior pastor.** What are you doing intentionally for personal growth? My *Leaders of Destiny Consulting* program can assist you in becoming the world-class leader God has called you to be.

2. **Grow your people.** What are you doing to intentionally grow the leaders around you? I have developed several leadership development programs to help your team push toward and achieve excellence.

I have written and said repeatedly, "Very few ministers and marketplace leaders have qualified and trained leaders around them." Yes, God wants to grow your business, church, and ministry beyond what you can even imagine (see Ephesians 3:20). Your organization will never get any bigger on the outside than the size of the leaders on the inside. For your organization to change, you and your leadership team have to change. For your organization to get better, you and your team have to get better.

LQ Solution: Leaders invest their time with solution-orientated people.

The million dollar question is: *Who are you anointing?* The problem-oriented people or the solution-oriented people? Pour the oil on the answer not the problem. Samuel anointed David (the solution) when Saul (the problem) was modeling poor leadership and giving God a fit. In my experience of working with pastors over the years, it seems that most leaders spend 80 percent of their time trying to pour oil on people who do not want to change and contribute nothing to the growth of the organization.

There are five kinds of people in every church:

1. Committed
2. Coming to Commitment
3. Complainers
4. Critical Cranks
5. Crazies

Most leaders spend 80 percent of their time with the complainers, critical cranks, and crazies. Why? The squeaky wheel gets the grease. Here is what I learned about the bottom three: they don't really want to change—they just want to be heard. The solution is to pour the oil on the committed and the coming to commitment. However, you cannot spend time pouring oil on them if you allow the complaining, critical cranks, and the crazies to take up your time. This requires a new way of thinking and a new way of working. Give 80 percent of your professional time to the committed and coming to commitment and only 20 percent of your time to the rest, committing personal time for family and yourself.

Two Mistakes Many Leaders Make

MISTAKE #1 – Putting people in leadership positions based solely on their potential. Ministry leaders often give people ministry positions based on a person's possibilities for future achievement instead of actual productivity. This is a big mistake. Somebody can have great talent, good looks, and incredible potential, but the question is, "Are they currently getting results in their own lives?"

For example, a business leader identifies both potential and proven achievement before hiring. The business person asks,

"You want a job as my personal assistant? Great! Then sit down at the table and let's see if you can type sixty to ninety words per minute." The business person is not going to hire someone who types twenty words a minute but believes he can type sixty words a minute in the future. No. They hire proven people who have already demonstrated the ability to perform at the desire level. So the employer asks, "Do you have relevant experience? Do you have a proven history of being a great personal assistant? Do you have professional references I can contact?"

LQ Solution: Potential positions a person to be developed and trained. Potential never qualifies a person for a leadership position.

In our church culture, we tend to get hyperspiritual about things and say, "If you have prayed about it and feel 'called by the Lord,' then here is a position for you." Achievement is measured by results. Past results are great indicators for future productivity.

MISTAKE #2 – Putting people in leadership positions who have not been both developed and trained. Natural talent and willingness to work hard for God doesn't qualify a person for leadership. They need to be developed and trained.

Church leaders often do not understand the difference between development and training. There is a difference between the need to be developed and the need to be trained. Development is all about internally developing the mind-set and attitudes of a leader. Development deals with your mental and emotional capacities. It involves knowing and understanding the skills necessary for self-mastery by knowing how to lead yourself first.

Training involves teaching specific tasks and equipping with particular skills that produce results. We must train people how to share their faith with others. Development produces a mind-set and motivation within a person to share the gospel. Training equips the person with practical "how-to steps" to actually witness, lead people to Christ, and disciple those people.

You have no idea where God will take you if you simply had the desire to be trained. What is the difference between a free dog you get at the dog pound versus a $18,000 champion you buy from a professional trainer? One word—training. One dog has been loved but has never been trained. Training is the difference maker to adding value to your organization and team.

LQ Solution:
Ministry Position - Proper Training = Frustration

Untrained leaders can have great attitudes and willing spirits but they often lack the practical training to do the job properly. If you see great potential in a person and simply give them a ministry position with no proper training, the result is frustration. When they do not do their job properly, you get frustrated with them. The person in the new position does not fully know what he is to do and what you expect from him, so he gets frustrated with you. Both of you are frustrated and neither one wants to talk about it.

LQ Solution: Underdeveloped and untrained leaders
become frustrated and frustrate others.

We do a great disservice to that person and to Christ when we put them into a leadership position without proper development and training. Every leader is responsible for developing and training those on their team. If you are frustrated with those working with or under you, look at yourself in the mirror and ask, "Did I offer this person the proper development and training so they can become who he or she is supposed to become? Have I established a culture that develops and trains leaders?" When we fail to develop and train others, we have no one but ourselves to blame for poor performance, lack of excellence, and no growth.

Leaders lose confidence in people when they don't do what they are asked to do. Then many leaders begin to believe the lie, "If I want the job done, I need to do it myself." This mentality paralyzes the leader in maximizing their impact, influence, and income. Trying to do everything, they do everything poorly. Effective leaders who achieve much for the Kingdom have discovered how to develop, train—and then delegate!

The Importance of Delegation

No one can aspire to leadership who does not delegate authority. This is the true test of leadership and also the prime compliment to those to whom responsibility and authority is delegated. Delegation is a confidence reward that says, "I believe in you. I trust you." Note carefully and seriously what these leaders say about delegation:

Learning to delegate effectively is even more important in determining the size of your contribution in life than your native intelligence is. –Bobb Biehl

The best executive is one who has sense enough to pick good people to do what he assigns them to do, and self-restraint enough to keep from meddling with them while they do it. –Theodore Roosevelt

I'd rather get ten men to do the job than to do the job of ten men. –D.L. Moody

I would rather something be done at 25 percent of my ability than wasting time giving 100 percent of my time doing it myself.

LQ Solution: Confident leaders have conquered the fear of delegation.

Why Leaders Don't Delegate

I've discovered six reasons why leaders don't delegate:

1. Fear of losing authority.

2. Fear of work being done poorly.

3. Fear of work being done better.

4. Not willing to take the necessary time required to develop and train those with potential.

5. Fear of depending on others.

6. Lack of personal training and positive experience.

Achievement that makes an impact will ultimately require you to develop, train, and then delegate. Each reason listed can be overcome with effective development and training of leaders. So, will you develop, train, and delegate to achieve lasting results, or will you continue to be busy and settle for frustration with minimal achievement?

Once you begin to unleash your LQ communication and equipping skills, you are ready to walk through L.E.A.D.E.R.S.H.I.P.

Unleash Your LQ

- Am I too involved in my church or organization?

- Can I pick up the phone and take a month off?

- Do I have a job or a ministry?

- Make a detailed list of all the things you do as a leader throughout a typical week.

- What are five things you need to put on your stop doing list?

- Who are the people you identified who are committed—or are becoming committed—to leadership in your church or organization?

- What are you doing to develop their potential?

- How are they being trained?

- Will you delegate and release equipped leaders?

- What fears keep you from delegating? How will you overcome these fears?

Endnote

1. Andy Stanly, *Next Generation of Leaders.*

YOUR LQ SOLUTION

WHAT IS
A LEADER?

For I have given you an example, that you should do as I have done to you. Most assuredly, I say to you, a servant is not greater than his master; nor is he who is sent greater than he who sent him. If you know these things, blessed are you if you do them.

–Jesus Christ

Gospel of John

Follow my example, as I follow the example of Christ.

–Saint Paul

1 Corinthians

CHAPTER EIGHT

LEADERS LEAD BY A POSITIVE EXAMPLE

Ask forty different people, "What is leadership?" You will probably get forty different answers. As a leadership expert, I thought it was important for me to come up with a standard definition for *leader* or *leadership*. I found there was no concise, universally accepted definition of a leader. In an effort to narrow the definition, I discovered there are many different facets of a leader; like a diamond, every time we turn it, we discover something different.

Acronyms help me remember principles. So in the following, each letter in the word *leadership* reveals an attribute. Throughout the remaining chapters, we will examine what this acronym tells us about leadership.

L —**Leads**
E —**Empowers**
A —**Attitude**
D —**Destiny**
E —**Excellence**
R —**Relationships**
S —**Security**
H —**Humility**
I —**Insight**
P —**Passion**

This chapter deals with the letter L, which tells us leaders lead by setting a positive example:

Let no one despise your youth, but be an example to the believers in word, in conduct, in love, in spirit, in faith, in purity (1 Timothy 4:12 NKJV).

To *lead* simply means to be out front. We are living in a day when there is a vacuum in leadership. When there is a lack of leaders in the world, something or someone will rush in and take up the space and fill the void. The current church focus on developing professional churchgoers rather than leaders has created a vacuum making it easy for the ungodly to move in and take over positions in every aspect of society. When there is a lack of godly leadership, people will follow anybody who is willing to get out in front. We need to realize our mistake of not developing leaders in our churches who work in the marketplace—and we need to implement a solution.

LQ Solution: We have good examples about how to behave in a church setting. Our challenge is to improve our example of behaving in the marketplace.

When Christian leaders display poor examples, we limit our level of impact, influence, and income. When the religious leaders in a community fail to be exemplary, the people in the culture lose trust in the voices of that community. Trust is the most important and powerful tool we have in our arsenal for effective leadership. If people lose trust in us, we lose the ear of our culture and ultimately our ability to lead.

The Bible contains stories of people's lives who produced both good and bad results. Wasn't God brilliant? We can learn from their good and bad examples, from both their failures and successes.

If you really want to learn how to lead and be successful, you have to reach for people who are where you want to be in life. Seek out successful people and learn from them. However, it is not always easy to get close to highly successful people.

If you can't get close to someone who is a success, go spend a day with a real failure. Take the time to sit down with somebody who has really messed up his or her life and ask the person:

- How did you get to this low point in life? (Whatever they did, don't do it!)

- What do you believe about leadership, money, and influence? (Whatever they believe, don't believe it.)

- What daily habits do you have? (Do the opposite.)

- What kind of books do you read? (Don't read those books.)

- What time do you get up in the morning? (Get up much earlier.)

- How much time do you spend watching television? (Watch less.)

At the end of the conversation, you need to say to yourself, *I'm not going to be like that!*

God gave us a Bible full of bad examples so we wouldn't become like them. We don't want to be like the ones who left a bad legacy behind. Ultimately, you will want to learn from both angles. You need to sit down with a person who is having great success and ask, "How did you do it?"

Everybody leaves behind some sort of legacy. Everybody will be remembered for the example they left behind—either good or bad. Make sure you are remembered as a good example. The most valuable gift a leader can give to his or her followers is a positive example.

But as He who called you is holy, you also be holy in all your conduct, because it is written, "Be holy, for I am holy" (1 Peter 1:15-16 NKJV).

It takes twenty years to build a reputation and five minutes to ruin it. If you think about that, you'll do things differently. –Warren Buffet

When I say the name Bill Clinton, what instantly comes into your mind? Monica Lewinsky. Nobody remembers that the American economy was good during his years in office. Nobody mentions the fact that he was the ultimate networker. He had a huge, fully-filled Rolodex™. He was a master networker who knew the importance of relationships. But—his bad character caused us to lose trust in him.

When I say the name Samson, what do you think? Delilah. We are not remembered for the good we have done. What sticks in the minds of people is that one bad thing we did. When people say your name, they will immediately think of that one stupid thing you did. It is hard to overcome a lapse of integrity.

God may not remember our bad deeds once we repent, but women do not have that ability. The first year we were married, I took my wife to a great restaurant for her birthday. I also bought her a beautiful gift. But the one thing I did not do was give her a birthday cake. Two months ago, after twenty years of marriage, she reminded me how I forgot to give her a birthday cake. Another good example about how people remember the one stupid thing we did—or forgot to do.

People's trust in leaders is at historic lows. People today are skeptical, cynical, and suspicious of anybody in leadership positions. Your ability to gain people's trust by building credibility as a leader empowers people to trust you with their heart and highest efforts.

LQ Solution: The minute you lose people's trust, you stop having the ability to lead them.

Integrity

Trust is earned. I am commanded to love you, but I am not commanded to trust you. Jesus trusted God, not men, because He knew what was in their hearts (see John 2:24). Trust is earned when leaders make right decisions. Right decisions made by leadership are like deposits in the bank account of trust within followers, and bad decisions are like withdraws in the trust account. When a leader makes more withdraws than deposits, their leadership ability ends or is in jeopardy. Their followers are bankrupt on trust. Remember that integrity is consistency in one's words and actions, trustworthiness, and true character.

LQ Solution: Lack of integrity fosters distrust and the inability to lead effectively.

A person's integrity becomes a prophecy of his or her destiny, just as the status of a farmer's field is a prophecy of the goods he will sell come harvest time. Choose to discount your integrity, and you will cheapen your destiny. Show me a person's character, and I can show you that person's future. We have to be very concerned with and model integrity to those around us. If we don't, we will lose their trust and will no longer be able to lead them.

He who walks with integrity walks securely [with confidence], *but he who perverts his ways will become known (Proverbs 10:9 NKJV).*

Choose to live according to divine principles, and you will alter your destiny for that which is good. It is your choice!

Adolf Hitler had influence, but it was bad influence. Lady Gaga has influence, but it is negative influence. We want to influence people to do what is right; that's Christian influence. So for me, I have got to focus myself as a leader to always do what is right. I also need to point out that there is a distinct difference between image and integrity.

LQ Solution: Integrity is who you are in private. Image is who you are in public.

Integrity is who you are in private. Integrity is who you are behind closed doors. Integrity is the decision you make when you are sitting in front of your computer and you are tempted to click the link that leads you to pornographic sites. Integrity is doing what is right even when you know the church people will not know what you did. The first person you have to lead is you. If you don't even trust yourself, you are sending off vibes that you cannot be trusted. You make these private decisions and you think you are getting away with them, but God sees all. Equally important, you see it, and you are whittling away your own trust. When you don't trust yourself, other people are not going to trust you. We are like radios sending off signal waves all over the place telling people how to treat us and whether or not to respect and follow us.

My wife travels with me probably 40 to 60 percent of the time. But sometimes I am alone in a hotel room. When I turn on the television, the first thing I see is this provocative picture telling me to watch these adult movies—and the title of the movie will not show up on the bill. Nobody will know. You might think there is no temptation, but that is not true. So what keeps me from pushing the button? I know the value of integrity. I always remember that I am not really by myself. God is always present! My own personal standard is high, so my integrity tells me I have to do what is right.

Image is who you project in public. Image is who you are up on the stage. Many people project a holier-than-thou image in church. However, behind closed doors they act like the devil. I don't ever want to project an "I am the holy man of God" image. I always tell people I have issues. Then they are more graceful to me when they see my mistakes.

We are living in a day when leaders think they can keep their private life separate from their public one. Many feel that their private life is none of anyone's business. Maybe true if you are a follower, but not true if you are a leader. Your private life will eventually become people's business. Ask Tiger Woods. Whether you like it or not, that is the price of leadership. And the higher you climb the leadership ladder, the more of your behind gets shown to everybody. You better have it covered.

Confidence, competence, and charisma may get you to the top, but character and integrity are what will bring you true and lasting success. Many leaders have confidence and competence, but they lack character. You have to guard your character and integrity at all costs. Don't go down in the history books setting a negative example like Bill Clinton, King David, Samson, or Tiger Woods.

Lead by Positive Example

The main principle of leadership is to lead by a positive example. Therefore, the leader's standard should always be higher than those of the followers. The apostle Paul set his leadership standard at the very top. He wrote, "Follow my example, as I follow the example of Christ" (1 Corinthians 11:1).

A survey conducted by an opinion research corporation for Ajilon Finance asked U.S. workers to select the one trait that was most important in a leader. Here are the results:

Rank	Leadership Characteristic	Percentage
1	Leading by Example	26
2	Strong Ethics or Morals	19
3	Knowledge of the Business	17
4	Fairness	14
5	Overall Intelligence and Competence	13
6	Recognition of Employees	10

As you can see from this survey, more than anything, people want leaders whose beliefs and actions line up. They don't want people who say one thing and live something totally different; they desire good examples who lead from the front.

LQ Solution: People do what people see. Leadership by example has the most powerful impact on followers.

We tend to think that our preaching and teaching from behind the pulpit is the key to developing leaders or disciples, but that is not true. Modeling leadership principles is the most powerful tool we have to develop leaders. This is the power of visualization. What we see modeled in front of us is the greatest sermon a leader can give. People become the images of what they see. Whatever you look at the most, you become. I find it interesting that opposites attract. However, if you look at a couple after they have been married twenty, thirty, or forty years, they start looking alike.

LQ Solution: Leadership is caught by the visual example people have in front of them every day.

The most powerful modeling you have had in your life was when you were a child. And the truth of the matter is, you are a whole lot like your parents whether you like to admit it or not. What people see in you affects them more than the sermons you preach to them or the lectures you give to them.

We have already learned that one of the quickest and easiest ways to naturally develop leaders is for leadership principles to be caught. The most powerful way you can impact people above you, around you, or under you is by your example or by modeling.

Do you know anyone who knows the whole Bible and tells you what you should do—but that person does not personally live out any of those values?

LQ Solution: Teaching is easy, but living out what you teach is the leadership challenge.

Norman Vincent Peale, author of *The Power of Positive Thinking* said, "Nothing is more confusing than people who give good advice but set a bad example." Therefore, nothing is more convincing than people who give good advice and set a good example. People will listen to people they like, but they will only follow people they trust.

We need more heroes, more leaders who will become something more than an average person. That is a hero—someone others can look up to and want to become like that person. People need a picture of who they could become. I want to emphasize again the importance of modeling as a leader.

The early followers of Saint Francis of Assisi wanted to know what to do when they took to the streets. "Preach the gospel at all times," Saint Francis advised. "If necessary, use words." Your everyday living is your real pulpit—where you really communicate the Gospel with others. The world is watching you, and looking at what your life is producing.

Let your light so shine before men, that they may see your good works... (Matthew 5:16 NKJV).

Unleash Your LQ

- Does your private life and your personal decisions line up with your public image? If not, why not?

- What options are you willing to surrender to be a better example of integrity to others?

- What aspects of your integrity must be eliminated or must improve for you to become more like Christ?

- What tempts you the most? How will you avoid and overcome that temptation?

Empower People

*In empowering people and teams, you learn new ways of
assessing people. The best part is watching employees become
associates. It's a lot of fun to "lead" them occasionally
to just a little bit more responsibility than they think
they can handle. Then when it turns out right and they
do handle it, it's great to see the pride in their faces.*

–Ken Blanchard and John P. Carlos
Empowerment Takes More Than a Minute

CHAPTER NINE

LEADERS EMPOWER PEOPLE

Leaders are master e-tank fillers. The e-tank, or the emotional tank, is like a gas tank. When the tank is full, you drive with confidence. Your team's emotions are also like that; if their e-tanks are full, they will perform with confidence and energy to get the job done. However, if their e-tanks are drained, morale drops through the floor, passivity sets in, and productivity starts declining. Then you scratch your head and wonder why your organization is plateauing or in decline.

A leader understands how to empower people so their e-tanks stay full. To empower people, you need to understand people. Empowerment creates momentum. When you have momentum, you look better than you really are. Without momentum, you look worse than you really are.

Empowerment means:

- Seeing the potential of an individual.

- Saying encouraging, empowering words to the person.

- Sharing your power and position and influence with the person.

- Showing others your belief in and power given to that person.

In the church we know a lot about doctrines. We have heard a multitude of teachings and sermons. I jokingly say, "Some of us have heard so many sermons, we are sermon possessed." We study the Bible to learn about God. However, leading an organization is more about your people skills than your great sermons or spirituality. If you desire to be a leader, you must understand what makes people tick—their psyche. Psychology is simply the study of human behavior based on how people think.

Church members often know much more about the vertical relationship with God than the horizontal relationship with others. Don't simply build spiritual disciplines, biblical knowledge, and understanding about God; you must also cultivate relational skills with people. Many people would like to stay locked up in their closet and have their "talk with Jesus," but they don't want to hang out in the coffee room and relate to others. As Charlie Brown says in Classic Peanuts, "I love humanity. It's people I can't stand."

LQ Solution: Your ability to develop better skills at connecting and developing relationships is the accelerator to help take you to where you need to go.

Do not buy in to the potential-destroying philosophy that you and God alone can do something big in the earth. If it is only you and God, you will only achieve a fraction of your potential. I can fail all by myself. I need a team of people around me to keep me on track. Build a team of people around you who will help get you to where you need to go.

Understanding people and developing people skills is the key to reaching where you need to be and becoming a better leader by empowering others. People are our most appreciable assets. The more you invest into other people's lives, the more return you receive. You can invest in megasize church buildings, multimillion dollar sound systems, laser beam lights, and coffee shops, which will all depreciate or break down in time. But when you invest your wisdom, time, and love into others, people appreciate, and they will eventually bring you a great reward.

You can take my factories, burn up my buildings, but give me my people and I'll build the business right back up again. –Henry Ford

A person's most important asset is people skills. Success is 87 percent people knowledge and 13 percent product knowledge.

LQ Solution: You can have people skills and not be a good leader, but you cannot be a good leader without people skills.

Understanding people is the LQ ability to discern why people do what they do, to know what people need, why they need it, and what you can do to empower others so that you will be seen as a leader.

Eight Important Things

There are eight important things that every leader should know about people to empower them:

1. ***People are insecure—so give them confidence.*** In the sea of a turbulent and insecure world, people are looking for an island of security to park their boats. People are looking for churches and businesses who provide an atmosphere of confidence. If you can provide it, they will come. A secure atmosphere is provided by secure and confident leaders.

Six things I know about people; most people:

- Are insecure and don't believe in themselves.

- Believe that no one has confidence in them.

- Can sense when you show honest confidence in them.

- Do whatever it takes to live up to the level of confidence you have in them.

- Never had anybody really believe in them.

- Are attracted, like magnets, to a person who has confidence in them.

LQ Solution: You can actually change people's lives by simply believing in them!

We have all heard this statement: You will never know what you can do until you try. But here is a lesser known statement: You will never try until you know what you can do. Great leaders give insecure people the confidence to know that they can do whatever God commands. Philippians 4:13 (NKJV) says, "I can do all things through Christ who strengthens me." This Scripture changed my life. When I first was saved and working in sales, I was having a long and terrible unproductive day. So I called my wife on the phone, and she told me to start claiming the verse: *I can do all things through Christ.* She encouraged me: "You can close this next sale; you can do this; you can finish this day strong!" Sometimes even the confidence coach needs a coach. Guess what? With a little checkup from the neck up, I was able to close one of my largest sales of the entire month.

We are in a daily battle against the FUD monster. Fear, Uncertainty, and Doubt can come on us at any moment. We need somebody to say, "Yes you can!" When you give somebody a pat on the back, you are giving the insecure, fearful, uncertain, and doubting person the confidence to know he or she can do it.

2. *People like to feel special—sincerely compliment them.* All of us love to feel special. What water is to a plant, encouragement is to the soul. Encouragement is a gift that keeps on giving. People need encouragement more than they need your criticism. The world is full of critics and dream destroyers.

Encouragement recognizes, accepts, affirms, and lets people know that they are valuable simply because they exist.

Most leaders and organizations spend most of their time telling people what they do wrong. How about rewarding people who do what is right and exemplify positive behaviors? You can empower people with confidence by rewarding them with gifts of encouragement, compliments, and appreciation.

One compliment can keep me going for
a whole month. –Mark Twain

The highest compliment a leader can receive is one given by a follower. However the highest compliment followers can receive is when the leader compliments them. When you compliment followers, that compliment does for them what the phone booth did for Clark Kent—aka Superman. Encouragement imparts a feeling of being special; and when people feel special, they are empowered. When people feel empowered, results show.

**LQ Solution: If you don't compliment and affirm
the people around you, you leave them wondering
how you feel about them.**

3. ***People are seeking a better tomorrow—show them hope.***
Hope is a confident expectation that my future is going to be my present. When you don't have hope for the future, you have no power in the present. The majority of the people in the world are hopeless. They have entered into learned hopelessness, which is the feeling that even though they have tried, nothing works, so why try any more. Leaders need to tell people that their future is way better than their present. The best days of their lives are just ahead of them, and encourage them to see their tomorrow is going to be better and brighter

than their present. A leader shows them that if they start expecting something better, they will become magnets for better relationships, better opportunities, and a better life.

**LQ Solution: Leaders tolerate the present,
but live in the future.**

4. *People need to be heard and understood—listen to them.* The Creator gave you two ears and one mouth. Why? Because He wants you to listen twice as much as you talk. Many times when someone comes to us with a problem, we have a tendency to want to fix everything. As soon as there is a problem, I want to fix it. Sometimes others don't want us to fix it—what they really want is for us to understand how they feel about the problem. The way we learn to understand what others really want and need from us is to really listen. Listening shows we care. Leaders listen.

*Listen to the whispers and you won't have to
hear the screams.* –Cherokee saying

Leaders learn to let others talk about themselves. A bad leader preaches sermons to people and dominates the entire conversation talking about him or herself. A great leader approaches a meeting with someone thinking, "What question can I ask that will reveal the four Hs—the person's head, heart, hurts, and hopes?" Great leaders ask great questions because it shows interest in the other person and that you want to understand them. Then they leave your presence feeling empowered.

The most empowering questions you can ask a person: "What do you think? How are you feeling? What would you do?"

5. *People need training—so spend time equipping them.* Disciples are disciplined ones. We will teach what we know,

but we will reproduce what we really are. Is your life worth reproducing?

Jesus' first twelve disciples were His inner circle. There were many other followers. Disciples were not the crowds that followed Him. Disciples were willing to learn what Jesus taught, then become a reproduction, and then reproduce what He was. We must spend time building our inner circle. In Bible days, it was common for a disciple to spend years being mentored and trained under a teacher.

Go therefore and make disciples… (Matthew 28:19 NKJV).

Learn the equipper's game plan: grow others and work yourself out of a job. When you work by yourself, like I tried to do when I thought I was Super Keith, you can only accomplish what you yourself can do. When you work on developing others, you multiply yourself.

Example:

Working by yourself: 3+3+3+3+3+3+3+3+3+3 = 30

Working through others: 3x3x3x3x3x3x3x3x3x3 = 59,049

When you work by yourself, you experience addition.

When you work together with a team, you experience multiplication.

Are you experiencing addition or multiplication?

---

6. ***People are selfish—so speak to their needs first.*** If you tell somebody they are selfish, they will probably get defensive and disagree with you. However, we all wrestle with selfishness. Let me prove it to you. When someone takes a picture of a group and they show you the picture, who do you look at first? We all look at ourselves and judge if we think the picture is good or bad based on how good we look in the picture. If you know people are selfish, then use that as a lever to move them

to where you need to go. This is not manipulation—this is knowing people and being sensitive to their needs.

When something should be changed in your organization, don't tell them what you want them to do for you. Remember, people are always thinking, "What's in it for me?" First, point out all the individual benefits to the members of your team. List as many benefits as you can possibly think of. Then tell them what you want to do and why. Finally, steer them where you want them to go.

7. *People get emotionally low—so encourage them.* Encouragement is to the soul what H_2O is to the body. The secret of success is to not let what you're doing get to you before you get to it. Be able to encourage and motivate yourself through the discouragement. It is the same with other people on your team. They need encouragement and power in their e-tank and a firm belief that they can do it.

When your team is discouraged, the fastest way I know to lift morale is to stop what you are doing and get your team to focus on past successes. Ask your team, "What are the top five accomplishments we have achieved over the past two years?" Eighty percent of the time your team will move from feeling discouraged to being encouraged.

Pay particular attention to increase your encouragement during times of change. Transition is a phase in which major encouragement needs to be your focus as a leader. In the middle of a transition, keep your team focused on their progress. Every transition causes an increase in the stress level (there is a predictable increase in stress because of increased indecision and lack of control), even though it may also represent major new opportunities as well.

8. *People desire meaningful relationships—so leaders provide community.* God's Word is all about community, from the

Garden of Eden at the beginning to the city at the end. People are looking for three Bs:

- **BEGIN**. Somewhere to begin anew.

- **BELONG**. For a place to belong.

- **BECOME**. A place to become something more than who they are right now.

Leaders give others a place to begin, belong, and to become— everyone wants those three things.

Church Survey:

Q. Why did you join the church?
A. Because of the pastor. (83 percent)
Q. If the pastor leaves, will you leave or stay?
A. "Stay," because they found friends at the church. (93 percent)

People seem to be living more segregated lives because of Internet relationships; but inside, they are still looking for real-life connections and relationships. I believe that Facebook will never replace one-on-one, heart-to-heart relationships.

Lyle Schaller has done extensive research that shows the more friendships a person has in a congregation, the less likely he or she is to become inactive or leave. In contrast, I once read about a survey in which they asked about 400 church dropouts why they left their churches. More than 75 percent of the respondents said, "It felt like no one cared whether I was there or not."

Leadership reproduces through equipping and empowering. Your job is to lead and to reproduce leaders. Identify now the ways you are equipping and empowering and what personal equipping you need to grow as you equip leaders.

Unleashing Your LQ

Examine your own leadership and rate yourself on a scale of 1 to 10 (10 being best) in the following behaviors:

1. _____ Do I convey confidence to others?

2. _____ Do I compliment people and make them feel special?

3. _____ Do I look for ways to offer hope to others?

4. _____ Do I listen to and understand the key people in my life?

5. _____ Do I know where I'm going and am I taking someone with me?

6. _____ Do I see things from the perspective of others and lead them accordingly?

7. _____ Do I encourage others and lift them up?

8. _____ Do I help people become more successful?

9. _____ Do I provide community where people can feel close to one another?

10. _____ Do I model for others a good example to follow?

The Impact of Attitude

Attitudes always impact a leader's effectiveness. President Thomas Jefferson remarked, "Nothing can stop the man with the right mental attitude from achieving his goal; nothing on earth can help the man with the wrong mental attitude."

–John Maxwell

Attitude 101

CHAPTER TEN

LEADERS HAVE ATTITUDE POWER

Attitude is the power behind every great leader in history. When I think of a leader, I think of someone who has a great attitude like the little boy sitting in the breakfast nook in his kitchen. He was drawing like crazy, and his mom looked over at him and asked, "Son, what are you doing?"

The boy said, "Mom, I'm drawing a picture of God."

His mother chuckled and said, "Of God? Son, nobody has ever seen God."

The young boy piped up and said, "They will when I'm done!"

Another little boy had a dream of becoming a professional baseball player. He was out in his backyard throwing the ball up in the air and trying to hit it. His dad was out trimming the bushes. He watched his young son throwing his ball up in the air, swinging the bat, and missing it time and time again. After about an hour, the father said, "Son, I know you have dreams of becoming a professional baseball player, but maybe you should consider another sport."

The young boy boldly shouted, "Dad, I may not be a great batter, but I will be the best pitcher that anybody has ever seen."

There was another young boy sitting in his kindergarten classroom. The assignment was to color a nice landscape. This young boy started drawing and coloring his picture. The teacher walked by and looked at his picture, noticing he had drawn flowers with smiley faces.

The teacher told the young boy, "Son, flowers don't have smiley faces."

The boy said, "Well mine do!"

That young boy's name was Walt Disney. There are smiley faces on every flower at the Disney parks because of what happened to him in kindergarten.

There are forces of negativity all around us, whether they come from our parents, leaders, or teachers. These forces of negativity are trying to move us out of being positive and confident and into negativity. When I think of a leader, I think of a person who has a great attitude. Such a person is able to remain positive even in a negative atmosphere and can even change that atmosphere from negative to positive.

Paul wrote the following Scripture while in a lower dungeon cell in a Roman jail. There he would have been in the midst of feces flowing down from the upper prison cells. It was dark and stinky and that is where he was when he wrote this verse:

Finally, brethren, whatever things are true, whatever things are noble, whatever things are just, whatever things are pure, whatever things are lovely, whatever things are of good report, if there is any virtue and if there is anything praiseworthy—meditate [think] *on these things (Philippians 4:8 NKJV).*

Dominate Your Thoughts, Control Your Attitude

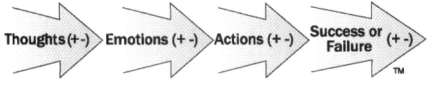

Thoughts (+ -) > Emotions (+ -) > Actions (+ -) > Success or Failure (+ -)

©KEITH JOHNSON, TheConfidenceCoach.com

When I think of leaders, I think of people who have learned to dominate their thoughts no matter what negativity they are facing. Your thoughts, whether they are positive or negative, are going to create emotions, and your emotions are going to create your behaviors, and your behaviors are going to create your results. So if your thoughts are negative, you will have negative emotions, which will in turn set in motion negative behaviors. If you behave negatively, you will get negative results in life.

Leaders are different from the negative, critical attitudes that dominate our culture. In the midst of negativity, they chose to think positively so their emotions are positive, which motivates them to behave in a proper manner in spite of the negativity around them. Therefore, they experience success instead of failure.

LQ Solution: Leadership is 20 percent talent, skills, and technical knowledge—and 80 percent attitude.

Your positive attitude can make up for your lack of:

- Education

- Money

- Beauty

- The right people connections

- Being in the right geographical location

- Physical stature

- Ability to write like a professional journalist

When I finished my first manuscript, we sent out thirty copies to different publishers. I will never forget the day my wife and I pulled up to the mailbox to get the mail and there was a big folder in our box. It was my first response from a publisher. When I opened the envelope, the letter said, "Mr. Johnson, we found your manuscript quite interesting and you did a wonderful job of laying out your points, but we are not interested in publishing your book."

Right away I said, "Great, praise God!"

My wife was looking at me thinking that a publisher accepted my book. I enthusiastically told her I had my first rejection. *Yes!* She looked at me like I was crazy. However, I knew that I had to go through some rejections to get to an acceptance. I received thirty rejections and responded to each one the same way. I know most people would have given up, but I refused to give up. I took control of my negative thoughts. I realized that maybe I just needed some coaching. I heard somebody say one time, "There are no shortcuts to success." I totally disagree! Coaching is definitely a shortcut to success.

I conducted some research and hired the best coaches in the book industry: Mark Victor Hansen and Jack Canfield, the authors of the *Chicken Soup for the Soul* series. I knew they had sold millions of books. They taught me what to do, and I did exactly what they taught me. When I sent out the next two new manuscript proposals, I instantly received two positive responses. As a matter of fact, both publishing companies started fighting over who was going to publish my book. *(See my Stop Dreaming and Start Writing Program in the Appendix.)*

Leaders fight through the negative rejections to get to the positives. You must maintain a positive mentality through the rejections because the truth is, you know that every *no* is leading you to your first *yes.* So you understand that crisis is simply an opportunity, and I use it as an opportunity to say, "Next." Try this, when somebody says, "No," you say, "Next." Some people look at a crisis as the end, but I say it is really the beginning. Some people look at the crisis as a failure. Leaders look at a crisis as an opportunity.

LQ Solution: Failure is not a person, it is only an event.

Here is a statement that will change how you think: *Failure is not a person, it is an event.* If you see it as an event, then you realize that we are failing our way to success. The average multimillionaire went bankrupt more than three times before achieving success. We all go through some events that don't turn out like we wanted them to turn out. But that does not make us failures. The only failures in life are people who don't try. Failing doesn't make you a failure. When God gives you a plan, you can't fail unless you quit.

If you try and move forward in an attempt to make your life better, you are a success. Losers don't even try. Don't label yourself a failure because you didn't get the outcome you wanted. Leaders see events from another perspective. What we call a crisis, God calls a classroom. Every failure event we have is a learning experience where we have the opportunity to add value to our lives. The things we learned from the mistakes we have made are what shaped us for where we are today.

Mental toughness is developed and revealed during the times of crisis, challenge, and change. Your attitude is never developed or revealed until you are put under severe pressure. Anyone can have a great attitude when everything is going great. Followers have positive attitudes when everything is going good for them, but as soon as something negative happens, the average person succumbs to the negativity. Remember you are called to lead, which means you are to become something more than the average person. So you have to make a decision that in the midst of negativity you are going to have a positive attitude so you can attain positive results.

LQ Solution: By persistence, the snail made it to Noah's ark.

What is the one characteristic of *all* successful leaders? They cultivate and possess an attitude of persistence! Persistence is the ability to keep going no matter what obstacles are placed in your way. Persistence is also the ability to face defeat again and again and not give up. It is the power to hold on, in spite of negative circumstances. Persistence is tenacity: *Hold on. Don't let go.*

It's a simple formula. Persistence = Action. The more action you consistently take, the closer you will be to attaining your desired outcomes in life.

Syndicated columnist Ann Landers wrote, "If I were asked to give what I consider the single most useful bit of advice for all humanity, it would be this: expect trouble as an inevitable part of life, and when it comes, hold your head high. Look it squarely in the eye, and say, 'I will be bigger than you. You cannot defeat me.'" This is the kind of attitude that leads to victory.

How Do You Respond in Crisis?

Ask yourself, "How do I respond in the midst of crisis?" Many people in the midst of crisis see it as the end of their life, or the end of their organization, or ministry, or business. What you call a crisis is really a launching pad to take you to the next level. Why? Because without a crisis, you would never think about making changes. Without change there is no progress in whatever you are doing. So we have to look at a crisis as an opportunity to move to a higher level.

Everybody today is complaining about the recession and the global economic crises and freaking out. I see these times as an opportunity, I can help others who may feel insecure and bring needed change into their lives.

Do you see a crisis as an opportunity or as the end? Do you label yourself a failure? Or do you say, "I am a success, and I am going to keep trying." Remember the proverb, be wise like the ant. If an ant comes up against an obstacle, it doesn't say, "I quit. It's the end." The ant finds a way around an obstacle no matter what it has to do.

How Do You Respond to a Challenge?

What is your attitude when challenges arise? David marched out onto the battlefield and he saw the challenge—Goliath. The average men were intimidated by the challenge. They saw the challenge as too big. But David saw the challenge from God's perspective. He saw how big his God was and realized how small Goliath really was. You have to look at challenges from God's perspective. Some people see challenges as mountains; others see ant hills. If you see a challenge as huge, you will never take the first step to move toward it. But even if you have an elephant-size challenge, eat the elephant one bite at a time.

Critics of Jesus criticized His optimism when He said that faith can move mountains (see Matthew 17:20). How can we move a mountain? One pebble at a time is all it takes. Mountains can be moved, but you have to start where you are. As a leader, you have to see the mountain you are facing as a molehill that you can conquer.

How Do You Respond to Change?

Your attitude is revealed in a time of change. Many people don't like change because change creates chaos. But the price of progress is change. If any organization is going to move forward over the next ten years, changes have to happen. If we will not change, we will not progress. Whatever does not progress becomes extinct. We will become as dinosaurs if we don't consistently change. Ten years ago cultural and informational change was happening every three years; today change is happening every six months. The only organization still holding on to old names, old ways of doing things, and the old way of operating is the church.

Your attitude is revealed when changes are made. Let me ask you:

* Do you embrace change?

* Do you love change?

- Are you a person who walks into a room and says, "What can we change? What can we do to make this better?"

- Or are you a person always fighting to keep the dinosaurs alive?

"This is the way we have always done it around here" is the greatest enemy of change. That is a negative attitude. That means you are living in yesterday. God is not in your yesterday. God is into your present and future. He is thinking about the future. We have to plan and strategize and look into the future and say, "Here is where we want to go." It's not enough to just see the future; a leader comes back to the present and says, "What changes do I have to make now so that the picture of the future can become a reality?" If we have negative attitudes about making changes, we will keep talking about change and saying things like, "One day we ought to...." Then ten years from now we find we are ineffective and irrelevant.

LQ Solution: Attitudes are contagious.
Is yours worth catching?

Take Control of Your Attitude

When you have a positive attitude, people will want to be around you. I have a friend who is always negative. He is negative about the economy, negative about everybody, and wonders why he doesn't have any friends. I have had so many people tell me they wish they had more friends. Birds of a feather flock together; you lie down with dogs and you are going to get fleas. But if you have a positive attitude, it will attract positive and successful people to you.

Every time you walk into any atmosphere, project a positive attitude and others will treat you in a positive way. Remember, attitude determines your altitude. It is going to shape how high you go in life. Attitude can't do everything for you, but it sure puts you on a journey to achieving a whole lot more in life.

In 1996, Heather Whitestone became the first handicapped Miss America. She was deaf. That was an amazing day because of what she achieved. Her dancing amazed the judges. She said, "I felt God when I was out there." It blew the entire crowd away. She is deaf, she can't hear music, but she dances. I saw her being interviewed on television one day. The interviewer asked her, "What is the greatest handicap a person can have in life?" She said, "The biggest handicap to a person's potential is a negative attitude." I agree. If you have a negative attitude, I am convinced even God can't help you.

Rise above the negative people around you. Move beyond the critical, pessimistic thinkers who squander possibilities and potential with their negative attitudes. Take every negative thought captive, rehabilitating them with the truths of God's attitude adjustment: *The plans I have for you are good—to give you a hope and a future!*

Unleash Your LQ

- Rate your attitude on a scale between 1 to 10 in the following areas: God, life, people, work, marriage, money, and the world around you. What bad attitudes do you need to work on?

- List every feeling you have about yourself and your Leadership Quotient. Are there more negative than positive feelings on your list? What will you think and do to eliminate the negative and focus on the positive?

- What negative people do you need to push out of your inner circle of friends? Which positive people do you need to begin walking with through life?

- After you read all my books, start reading books by Norman Vincent Peale, Robert Schuller, and Joel Osteen. Memorize the book of joy in the Bible—Philippians.

Vision

The first step toward creating an improved future is developing the ability to envision it. VISION will ignite the fire of passion that fuels our commitment to do WHATEVER IT TAKES to achieve excellence. Only VISION allows us to transform dreams of greatness into the reality of achievement through human action. VISION has no boundaries and knows no limits. Our VISION is what we become in life.

–Tony Dungy, Nathan Whitaker,
Denzel Washington
Quiet Strength

CHAPTER ELEVEN

LEADERS ARE DESTINY DREAMERS

The whole secret of a successful life is to find
out what it is one's destiny to do,
and then do it. –Henry Ford

I spent most of my adult life being a leader of history. Why? Let me explain: I grew up very poor. My stepfather worked in construction. There were years when he went without any work and money for months at a time. We lived in an average-sized home way out in the country. However, I lived only a few miles from some of the most influential and financially prosperous communities in Fort Wayne, Indiana. Because of our location, I went to school with the "rich kids" who lived in the biggest homes, drove the nicest cars, and wore designer clothes from expensive stores. Eventually most of the "rich kids" became my friends, and I would go over to their big, beautiful homes to play and study.

My best friend's dad was a well-known doctor in our city. Every time I visited, I was amazed at the size of his home. The refrigerator was always full of food and the cupboards full of snacks. And he had so many toys! I remember thinking, *I don't want to be like my parents when I grow up! I want to be rich like this doctor.* Consequently, I have been driven to succeed most of my life.

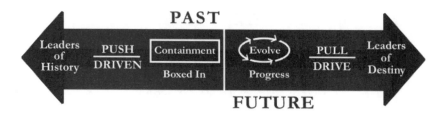

Doesn't this sound like the making of a great success story? Well, not so fast. As illustrated in the graphic, I was actually being "driven" by my past and not allowing destiny to give me "drive" for the future. I have now realized that I was driven by the fear of ever being a failure or poor again. *Fear was pushing me rather than destiny leading me with confidence into the future.*

What has driven you to this place of success at this point and time in your life?

LQ Solution: Leaders of *history* are driven by the past.

The fear of failure and poverty "push" some to achieve some levels of success. When a leader is being pushed by fear, he or she could be tempted to do unethical things to succeed. Leaders of history tend to live unfulfilled lives of regret. When a leader is driven by the past, this can become a very unhealthy situation.

WARNING! This is the reason many high-profile, successful ministry people have fallen. Most have come from a family background of struggle and poverty. Therefore, they are highly tempted to compromise their integrity in fear of living in poverty again.

LQ Solution: Leaders of destiny get their drive from the "pull" of the future—fulfilling their life purpose and destiny.

Leaders of destiny have a life purpose that is fueled by dream energy. Leaders of destiny have evolved. They have experienced the transformational shift in their minds from *wanting success* to *having a passion for significance* by becoming a patriarch and leaving a legacy. Leaders of destiny enjoy a life of fulfillment as they journey forward into their future. When a leader's drive comes from destiny, that leader is emotionally, mentally, and spiritually healthy.

What Is Destiny?

Destiny asks the question, "What does the picture of your future look like?" Destiny is the beginning process of inventing or reinventing a person, church, or organization. Most people and organizations trap themselves in an old identity and never update who they are today and who they are to become in the future.

Many people view the word "destiny" as some sort of mystical term that does not apply in the marketplace or ministry. In reality, your destiny is a preview of your future potential. Destiny begins as photographs, expectations, and hopes within our hearts and minds—things that we want to accomplish in our future. Your heart beats to the rhythm of your destiny. It's the song that gives your life motion and the vision that propels you forward. Your destiny gives purpose to your steps. Everyone has a destiny, but not everyone walks the path to fulfilling it.

Destiny is seeing with the mind's eye what is possible for you, your organization, in other people, in projects, and in enterprises. Destiny represents God's desires, dreams, hopes, goals, and plans for the future especially for you. Destiny is about unlocking and using your imagination to create a future you desire.

Destiny is:

- The imperative to exchange a life for a moral cause that will endure.

- To be awakened to the opportunity to become something more than what you are right now.

- To see something you have never seen before.

- New possibilities. Once your eyes are open to the ultimate plan for your life or organization, you begin to experience transformation in your thoughts, emotions, energy levels, and actions.

- The end result of the magnificent plan for your life.

Destiny Trumps Your Past!

We are asleep with compasses in our hand. –Poet W.S. Merwin

Destiny is greater than history, greater than the failures of the past, greater than discouragement, and greater than the emotional scars of the past. When you are awakened by destiny, you are empowered to see the pathway that will lead you to a brand-new destination. While the word "destiny" is not used in the Bible, the cumulative impact of destiny is defined in Ephesians 2:10, "For we are God's masterpiece. He has created us anew in Christ Jesus, so we can do the good things he planned for us long ago" (NLT).

When you *don't* have a sense of destiny or vision for the future, you tend to fall prey to the human tendency toward learned hopelessness and victimization. However, destiny is the daily fuel that empowers you with the ability to exercise patience, persistence, and perseverance in order to achieve your dreams.

The future belongs to those who see possibilities
before they become obvious.
–John Sculley, former CEO of Pepsi and Apple Computer

Destiny points you and your organization in the right direction. One of the main reasons why leaders do not have "leadership confidence" is because they cannot see where they want to go in the future. Destiny is not about setting goals. Most churches and companies set goals they want to reach each year. There is a drastic difference between setting a goal and being driven by a personal commitment toward a destiny. Destiny always points to something bigger and better in the future. Destiny should be so big that it requires extraordinary team effort. Destiny should also be so large that it will require ten to thirty years of effort to complete.

Ten years from now you are going to arrive. The question is where? Leaders of destiny know exactly where they want to go and they consistently move toward it.

LQ Solution: Leaders don't wait for destiny to show up; they receive it and then create it.

Destiny in the Heart of a Leader

The leadership process of turning a dream into reality begins with a deposit of destiny in the heart of a person to solve a major problem or meet an immediate need.

Jack Welch took over as the CEO of General Electric (GE) during a time when the company was facing some major challenges. This leader of destiny totally turned GE around. He stated that the first step, before all other steps, was for the company to "define its destiny in broad but clear terms. You need an overarching message, something big, but simple and understandable."[1] What was the biggest problem General Electric was really facing? Apparently the lack of a clear destiny. Jack Welch and GE came up with a statement of destiny when they set the following goal:

"To become #1 or #2 in every market we serve and revolutionize this company to have the speed and agility of a small enterprise."[2]

Armed with a profoundly simple, clear, and compelling destiny, Jack Welch led GE into a new and prosperous future.

At forty-three years of age, Henry Ford wanted to improve transportation beyond the slow pace of a horse and buggy. He also wanted to meet an immediate need of producing a car that every person could afford and own. Henry Ford led his company forward with destiny burning in his heart to "democratize the automobile." He said: [To] build a motor car for the great multitude...It will be so low in price that no man making a good salary will be unable to own one—and enjoy with his family the blessing of hours of pleasure in God's great open spaces...everybody will be able to afford one, and everyone will have one. The horse will have disappeared from our highways, the automobile will be taken for granted.[3]

One of the greatest examples of destiny is Sony's vision in the 1950s for its future:

We will create products that become pervasive around the world...We will be the first Japanese company to go into the U.S. market and distribute directly...We will succeed with innovations that U.S. companies have failed at—such as the transistor radio...Fifty years from now, our brand name will be as well known as any in the world...The name Sony will signify innovation and quality that rival the most innovative companies anywhere.... "Made in Japan" will mean something fine, not something shoddy.[4]

Like Jack Welch, Henry Ford, and Sony, ignited by a destiny that was simple, clear, and compelling, your vision for a bigger and better future will serve as a unifying focal point of productivity and achievement, ultimately creating immense team spirit.

You do not have to be a charismatic leader to build a great organization for the future. However, you do have to be a leader who imagines the possible and understands how to inspire and motivate others.

Imagine what is possible; believe it is possible for you!

To ignite a destiny requires you to think the unthinkable. You can increase your leadership confidence by using your imagination. All creation begins in the imagination, which is the primary source for creating change and the incubator of all ideas that eventually make their way into reality. Your imagination creates and preplays pictures of things you want to happen in your future. Visualize now what your achievements in the future are going to look like. Your imagination is an invisible factory machine inside your mind waiting to produce the photographs of the future you desire to create. Through your imagination, you can visualize and create a beautiful, undeveloped future that is in line with your true potential.

Consider a destiny with an impact so dynamic that it will last at least one hundred years after you have expired. Your destiny should be a massive broad stroke of what your future will look like—it should not be measurable.

Are You a Leader of Destiny or a Leader of History?

Leaders of *destiny* are future focused. They look through the front windshield as they drive forward on the journey to making their dreams come true. Leaders of destiny ask questions such as:

- Where are we going?
- When are we going to get there?
- What are we doing?
- Why are we doing it?

- Are we getting results?

- What are we going to do when we get there?

Do you find yourself asking these types of questions on a regular basis? If so, this book alleviates your concern that you are "crazy" just because you despise mediocrity and the status quo.

Leaders of *history* are past focused. They make these types of statements: "Where have we been? Why change? We have always done it this way. What we are doing is working. I'm so busy, I don't have time think about or plan for the future. Remember how it used to be?" Do you find yourself making some of these same statements on a regular basis? If so, this book will give you the tools you need to transition from a leader of the past to a leader of destiny.

Leaders of destiny spend more time thinking about the future and less time thinking about the past. The one thing we can do about the past is learn from it, *but the lessons are valuable only if they are applied to the future.*

Leaders of destiny forecast trends, envision scenarios, initiate positive changes, and help create the desired future. Great leaders only tolerate the present—they live in the future. After Walt Disney's death and then the completion of Disney World, someone said, "Isn't it too bad Walt Disney didn't live to see this?" Mike Vance, creative director of Disney Studios replied, "He did see it—that's why it's here."[5]

Vance understood how Disney envisioned the future. It was Walt Disney himself who said, "The future is not the result of choices among alternative paths offered in the present—it is a place that is created first in the mind and will; created next in activity."

LQ Solution: Leaders turn their destiny and dreams into a plan. Dream - Plan = Fantasy

Some people say that desperate times demand desperate actions. I disagree. I say that desperate times demand strategic planning. For the past three years of this economic crisis, I have been busier than ever consulting and helping pastors with strategic planning for the future. With the exception of one pastor who did not follow his own plan, every pastor experienced spiritual, numerical, and financial increase.

Leaders of destiny understand the importance of turning their vision into a strategic plan. Many people have great dreams, goals, and desires for a better tomorrow. However, many of these dreams, goals, and desires will never come to pass unless you develop a strategic plan and then work the plan. Your destiny tells you where you want to go; your dreams and goals tell you when you want to get there; and a strategic plan tells you how you are going to do it. As a leader, you must turn your destiny, dreams, and goals into a written strategic plan.

Leaders of destiny know that hoping and wishing is not a strategy. They know that a vision without a strategic plan is only a fantasy, and that they cannot be strategic if their efforts lack context.

A fool with a plan can outsmart a genius with no plan.
–T. Boone Pickens, Texas billionaire and successful businessman

Surprisingly, I have found that very few businesses, colleges, nonprofit organizations, television stations, and churches have detailed written plans for their future. Many organizations have a one-year plan or a one-year budget, but few have a detailed ten- to twenty-year plan. In my own personal observations, only about 5 percent of churches, companies, and organizations have such a plan. Of the 5 percent that do have a strategic plan, they are also listed as the top 5 percent in their field. Interestingly, I have found that 95 percent of all project failures are the result of improper planning.

Why don't more people and organizations plan for the future? Because planning is not easy. If planning was easy, everybody would be doing it based on the results it produces. I don't like planning myself. However, I discovered that planning can be easy if I have the right tools to help me in the process.

The Destiny Arrow is a tool designed to help you make the planning process easy, quick, and fun. This fourteen-step coaching process helps take your church to the next level and beyond. *(For more information see Appendix C.)*

LQ Solution: Your personal or organizational history will become a snapshot of your future unless you embrace change in your present.

The next sea of change is upon us. We must recognize this change as an opportunity to take our offerings to the next level.... –Bill Gates, cofounder and chairman, Microsoft

The Curse of Sameness

Leaders of history are content where they are and contentment breeds containment. Sameness is the ball and chain that keeps a leader locked up in limitations. Staying the same can become a curse. Native American Indians understood this quite well. If they did not like someone, they would curse the person by saying, "May you stay in the *same* place." When they said this, they were obviously thinking about more than geography. They were wishing a stagnant personal journey, a family that would not grow, a future that was less than prosperous. They were wishing that the person would remain in the same condition, without moving, without growing, and without changing. Remaining stagnate produces mediocrity, regret, and an unfulfilled life.[5]

LQ Solution: Leaders of destiny continually strive to stay ahead of the game.

Leaders in the twenty-first century must evolve or die. We cannot assume that just because something works today, it will continue to work tomorrow. While the concepts of growth and change have been studied for years, in actuality, both are occurring at a much faster rate than ever.

The *Leaders of Destiny* book and our companion *Destiny Arrow* consulting program empowers you to stay ahead of the game, to maximize your leadership effectiveness, and evolve from a leader of history to a leader of destiny. Decide now to change your leadership focus from the urgent and immediate to the long-term impact you are moving into as you journey toward your destiny.

Unleash Your LQ

- Do you have a clear picture of your future? If not, why not?
- Ask yourself the seven LQ questions:

  1. *Destiny: Where am I going?*

  2. *Purpose: Why am I here?*

  3. *Identity: Who am I?*

  4. *Past: Where did I come from?*

  5. *Potential: What am I capable of?*

  6. *Plan: How am I going to do it?*

  7. *Legacy: What do I want to leave behind and how long?*

Endnotes

1. Noel M. Tichy and Stratford Sherman, *Control Your Destiny or Someone Else Will* (New York: Doubleday Currency, 1993), 245-246.
2. Robert Slater, *The New GE* (Homewood, IL: Richard D. Irwin, 1993), 77-93.
3. Daniel J. Borstin, *The Americans: The Democratic Experience* (New York: Vintage Books, 1974), 548.
4. Keith Johnson, *Leaders of Destiny* (Spring Hill: KJI Publishing, 2009).
5. Samuel Chand, *What's Shakin' Your Ladder*, 148.

Seek Excellence

If a man is called to be a street sweeper, he should sweep streets as Michelangelo painted or Beethoven composed music, or Shakespeare wrote poetry. He should sweep streets so well that all the hosts of heaven and earth will pause to say, "Here lived a great street sweeper who did his job well."

–Dr. Martin Luther King Jr.

There is no traffic jam on the extra mile.

–Zig Ziglar

CHAPTER TWELVE

LEADERS POSSESS A SPIRIT OF EXCELLENCE

The word "excellence" comes from the root word "excel," which means to go and thrust beyond. A leader is an average person who has chosen to do more than what the average person has done so that others will look to him or her and want to follow. When I think of a leader, I think of a person who thrusts beyond what the common person is doing and becomes something more valuable.

Proverbs 22:29 reads, "Do you see a man who excels in his work? He will stand before kings; he will not stand before unknown men" (NKJV).

Reading that verse years ago, I realized that God was preparing me to speak to royalty because a man who excels in what he does is not going to hang out with ordinary people. He is going to hang out with extraordinary people. In order for me to prepare myself, I had to realize God had destined me for something much bigger than where I was. I had to lift my personal standard of what I expected out of my future.

LQ Solution: Life will never change until we lift our own personal standard of what is acceptable and begin to really grasp the magnitude of what God is preparing us for.

I was awakened to the fact that God was preparing me to change nations, powerful businesses, and companies by changing the leaders of major organizations. If God was going to use me, I knew I had to get ready. I had to lift my standard to a higher level and become more than who I was. At this time of my life, I thought I was really doing my best work. However, I realized my best could get even better, and I had to continue the process of pushing myself to be better.

Three examples of excellence that inspire me in the Bible:

1. God is Excellent. Creation confirms a job well done. *"O Lord, our Lord, how excellent is your name in all the earth!* (Psalm 8:1)

2. Jesus is Excellent. He made sure He did all things well. *"And they were astonished beyond measure, saying, 'He has done all things well...'"* (Mark 7:37 NKJV).

3. Daniel was Excellent. He pushed himself to be the best in the world. *"And in all matters of wisdom and understanding about which the king examined them, he found them **ten times** better than all the magicians and astrologers who were in all his realm...because an **excellent** spirit was in him"* (Daniel 1:20, 6:3 NKJV).

Daniel is a model of a leader of cultural transformation. He impacted his country. He had influence in government. He was highly educated, schooled in both Hebrew and Babylonian thought. And he had wealth to back him up. Daniel was a man of great impact, influence, and income who rose to the top to become a leader of leaders.

Daniel was superior to everyone else because of his passion for excellence; he became ten times better than all the magistrates and all the astrologers in the land. Think about this, when Daniel was two times better than everybody else, to whom did he have to compare himself? Nobody. What about five times better or ten times better? Again, nobody! Daniel reached the top of the Leadership Advancement Mountain. He became the head and not the tail. At the top, you can't compare yourself to anybody else.

So who are you in competition with? Yourself! You are in competition with yourself to excel and be the best at what you do.

Daniel's secret—he never allowed comparisons, contentment, or satisfaction with his current achievements to limit his potential. He was passionate about continual improvement.

I was fortunate to do some speaking and training for one of South Africa's wealthiest business owners. At dinner, I pulled out my yellow notepad and asked him what his secret for success was. He gave me two simple yet profound points:

POINT 1 – His commitment to honor God and His Word in everything they do.

POINT 2 – His company's commitment to excellence in how they treat employees, product development, and customer service.

Then my friend said, "My company has established such a reputation with the government officials that they know if I present a proposal for contracted work, it will be done with the utmost excellence. In all my years in business I have landed 100 percent of the government job proposals I have applied for in my nation."

LQ Solution: Excellence is using the money, time, and resources you have and maximizing them to your best ability.

Let's face it. Each new level of excellence is going to cost you money. Excellence is not cheap. Excellence is expensive. Reaching a level of excellence is different for everybody based on your cash flow. If you pastor a small church in a rural country area with a limited budget, but you have taken that money and used it to produce the best possible excellence in all that you do, you may not have a Starbucks in your foyer or a $500,000 light show, but you are operating in excellence. I have been in large churches with thousands of people and huge budgets, yet everything about the outside and inside of the building is outdated and lacks the feeling of freshness and excellence.

I have a pauper's budget but I used what I do have to make my small home feel like a king's palace. –Hennie Goodman

LQ Solution: Excellence = Influence + Impact + Income
Mediocrity = Sameness + Shame

LQ Solution: Today's excellence becomes tomorrow's mediocrity.

Since excellence is the passionate pursuit of improvement, today's excellence becomes tomorrow's mediocrity. When we believe we did our best today, if we do the same thing tomorrow, then tomorrow becomes mediocre. Most people stay satisfied with their current performance, not realizing that if they don't continually improve they are settling for the commonplace. We have to continually say, "Lord, I want a heart of excellence."

Excellence will take you to the top because mediocrity is common. It is common to do everything mediocre, but it is uncommon to make a decision to do things with excellence.

LQ Solution: Smart leaders leverage the "WOW Factor."

If you are going to be excellent, then you have to do the "extra." If you are going to be extraordinary you must do the "extra," not the common. An old, beige, banged up Toyota Camry captures nobody's attention as it cruises through town. But what happens if a fire engine red Lamborghini drives through town? Everybody on the street takes a second look and says, "WOW!" Yes, both cars will get you from point A to point B, but the common car goes through the streets unnoticed making no impact or influence on the pedestrians.

If you are going to be a person or a ministry of excellence, you have to WOW people. We are to let our light shine! God doesn't want us to go through life like the old, beige, Toyota Camry, invisible and unnoticed. Mediocre people, ministries, and businesses are invisible. You are called to be the Lamborghini that WOWs everybody. People should see you operating at excellence and say, "Wow! How did you achieve this level of success and excellence? I want to do the same thing."

I was on the phone the other day; someone called to ask me about speaking at a leadership conference. "Wow, you are America's number one Confidence Coach?" My reply, "Who do you want, number two?" Nobody wants to hear number two, they want the best.

Want the WOW Factor to operate in your life? Start by setting a higher standard for yourself and say, "I want to become the very best at what I do. I want to operate at a world class status!" Now, all you have to do is the EXTRA.

I teach pastors everywhere I go that it is easy to have an excellent church. All you have to do is master how you train the greeters at the front doors. Most churches are average. They have some old guy at the door wearing a polyester suit with a tie that looks like it was made in the 1950s. He says, "Come on in. Welcome to our church." When guests ask him how to get to the sanctuary, he simply points in the general direction. How average is that? What kind of a first impression is that?

Today, people decide whether they are coming back to church in the first five minutes of arriving at your facility. Being a greeter is a great opportunity to display the excellence of a church. Treat people like they are worth a million dollars. Instead of having just one person greeting, have ten to twenty people in the foyer welcoming people and making them feel comfortable. Go beyond what the average church does, and visitors will say, "Wow! This is the Lamborghini, not the boring, beige Camry."

LQ Solution: Excellence is all about the extra.

Do the extra. Think about the assignments that you have been given and ask yourself, "How can I do my assignment a little bit better and go beyond average to greatness?"

The Rebecca Principle

Abraham sent his chief servant to find the bride for his son Isaac. The servant was sent out with a large entourage of camels loaded down with all kinds of good things from his master. When he came to a well just outside town, he met a woman named Rebecca (see Genesis 24:12-14). She offered to draw water for him to drink and then she said, *"...I will draw water for your camels also, until they have finished drinking"* (Genesis 24:19 NKJV).

These days we don't have camels, but we do have dogs, and if they need a drink of water, we go to the sink and fill their water bowl at the faucet. However, in our Bible story, the servant had ten camels (vs. 10), and one camel can drink twenty gallons of water for one drink. With a five-gallon jug and ten camels, each one needing to drink twenty gallons of water, Rebecca had to draw 200 gallons of water. She had to drop the jug down in the well, then pull it up full of water—five gallons at a time to give the camels a drink. She had to make forty trips to the well and lift over 2,000 pounds of water. It would have taken her nearly half a day. Do you think she was a little sore the next morning? Rebecca went beyond mediocre; she did the extra.

People today want to exhibit minimum effort and receive maximum benefits. Rebecca was the opposite. She gave maximum effort for minimum expectation.

> *Excellence is doing a common thing in an uncommon way.* –Booker T. Washington

LQ Solution: Leaders give the maximum effort even when only the minimum is expected.

Want greater results? Apply the Rebecca Principle and get extraordinary results. Remember that Rebecca was chosen to be Isaac's wife. Excellence will always bring you to a place of sweet promotion.

Leaders See What Others Fail to See

> *Heaven and Earth were finished, down to the last detail.* —*Genesis 2:1 MSG*

Excellence is all about paying attention to the details that give rise to superior performance, which leads to promotion in life. God is a great leader; therefore, He paid attention to every detail when He created the heavens and the earth. He left nothing undone!

God also paid attention to all the details when He created the human race. If God had created your nose upside down, when it rained, you would drown. Because God paid attention to details, He made sure all of our body parts were in the right place and functioned to serve their purposes as part of the whole body.

Leaders understand that in order to be excellent they must pay attention to the details. Paying attention to the details is the key to becoming a person who stands out in a crowd and others will look toward. Leaders pay close attention to what others seem to ignore.

LQ Solution: The rewards in life always go to the person who is able to see the little details that the majority seem to overlook.

Excellence – The Power to Change the World

Similarly, you cannot grow your maximum potential if you continually work outside of your strength zone. Improvement is always related to ability. The greater your natural ability, the greater your potential for improvement. I've known people who thought that reaching their potential would come from shoring up their weaknesses, and so they never developed their strengths. But do you know what happens when you spend all your time on your weaknesses and never develop your strengths? You reach mediocrity, but never attain excellence. Nobody admires or rewards mediocrity.

Only your best will add value to others and lift them up. –Dr. John Maxwell

LQ Solution: Excellence is produced by focusing on your strengths.

The attitude of excellence you want to set as a leadership team in your church is for the team to say, "This is such a great church, why would we think of going anyplace else?" versus, "Do we have to go to church today?" The goal of a business should be, "This company treats us so good, why would I want to work anywhere else? This company gives us such great service, why would I want somebody else?" The goal of an employee should be, "I will do more than my boss expects. I will be so good at what I am assigned to do that I will not have to worry about getting a pink slip." Now, let's turn our attention to the final letter in Leader and focus on "relationships."

Unleash Your LQ

- What three changes could improve your quality of work by 50 percent in the next month?

- What strengths are you working on now to develop?

- Which details have you been overlooking that must be addressed immediately?

- Describe a current situation that needs you to employ the Rebecca Principle.

Relationships Are Everything

A wise youth minister many times said, "To God, relationships are everything." We are created for meaningful, abundant lives in communion with God and others. By design, our greatest fulfillment begins when we enter a relationship with God through Jesus Christ. That primary relationship enables us to develop healthy, satisfying relationships with others. Our daily tasks are more attainable when we can share the load. Equally rewarding, we get to return the favor, to lift up someone who falls or needs encouragement. God's best gifts come in relationships.

–Judi Mayne
"Relationships Are Everything" in
Faith in the Workplace, Seattle Pacific University

CHAPTER THIRTEEN

LEADERS VALUE RELATIONSHIPS

When I think of a leader, I think of those who understand, protect, and value the power of relationships. As mentioned previously, some say, "There are no shortcuts to success." I disagree. Relationships, which include coaching, are the shortcuts to your future success and the doorways to a bright tomorrow.

You don't really decide your destiny; you decide your relationships, and your relationships are what ultimately decide your future. Every season of your life is marked by a new person coming into your life. The exit from one season to the next season is a person.

Ruth's life changed from one season to the next season when she connected with Naomi. Ruth's life changed drastically again when a wealthy business owner named Boaz entered her life. You are only one person away from a change of seasons in your own life. When God wants to promote you, He brings the right person into your life. When the enemy wants to destroy you, he brings the wrong person into your life. That is why you must have wisdom. Wisdom is the ability to discern right and wrong (see Proverbs 2). You need to get understanding so you can increase your discerning ability. Who is the right person and who is the wrong person for your advisor, mentor, or friend?

Your environment has to be right for your wisdom to be right. Wrong environments create wrong decisions. You change a person's life by changing their environment. Have you ever had fish as "pets"? If so, you may have noticed that if one fish gets sick, the rest of the fish get sick, too. If you take the fish out of that environment and put it in another bowl, the fish is shocked and dies anyway. Rather, you have to cleanse the environment that the fish is in. Eliminate the sickness by removing the contaminated water. Likewise, one person on your team can contaminate the entire environment.

LQ Solution: True leaders influence their environment more than their environment influences them.

You have to look discerningly at the relationships in your life because your relationships are either pointing you toward your destiny or away from it. Show me a person's relationships, and I will show you that person's future. Leaders reach for relationships that are where they want to go. Stop hanging out in toxic environments with people who are going nowhere.

When people tell me everybody is affected by this recession and everybody they know is struggling in some way I say, "That's funny, because everybody I know is having the best years of their lives." I tell them that they need to reconsider who they are hanging out with. If everybody around you is struggling, what does that tell you about the quality of relationships you have? You need to cleanse your environment. You need to reach for people who are where you want to go, and disconnect from those old relationships.

Connect to relationships that are going somewhere, that inspire you to dream, inspire you to believe bigger, and motivate you to act. You may need to find new friends and colleagues.

When you get around new people you will:

- See new possibilities
- Think bigger thoughts
- Hear new messages
- Take positive actions

Relationships are the key to accelerating your destiny. It is of the utmost arrogance to say, "All I need is God to succeed." You need people to help you get from where you are to where you need to go. I value my relationships more than money. I can lose all my money, but if I keep my relationships, I can always get more money. I will always have the ability to rebuild.

I don't get involved with network marketing businesses. I travel worldwide and someone always tries to get me involved in their new and upcoming network marketing business. The promises of million dollar checks are appealing. However, the opportunity may bring me short-term prosperity, but what happens if this business fails? All those valuable relationships I involved in my network are possibly lost forever. Then I have lost my greatest wealth.

LQ Solution: Your network determines your net worth.

I need my high quality relationships to help me get to where I need to go. If I lose those, then I have to start all over at ground level. Wealthy and successful-minded people place a high value on relationships. This is why really wealthy people can build multibillion dollar businesses, lose it all, then spring right back up. They have developed the relationships necessary to get more capital to build it up again.

You Need Four Crazy Friends

You need four crazy friends in your life who refuse to allow you to quit. Remember the story in the Bible about the paralyzed man whose four friends were trying to bring him to Jesus for healing? Jesus was in a full house and there was no room to get in. Now some nice, normal, easy-going friends would have given up saying, "Forget it; Jesus is too busy." But this man had four crazy friends who decided they were not going to allow their paralyzed friend to lie there until he died. They refused to allow him to lose.

They were willing to do something crazy to help their friend. They were willing to step out of the norm and get him to Jesus. They were determined to win. They carried their friend up to the roof, tore a section of the roof away, and dropped him down right in the middle of the positive atmosphere around Jesus (see Mark 2:1-6).

You have a choice: Will you be persistent and prosperous, or passive and poor? You need some friends in your life who will get in your face and tell you there is more inside of you. Such friends will continually tell you that:

- You are a champion—not a chump.

- You are a winner—not a loser.

- You are going over—not under.

You need some crazy friends who dare to believe in you against all perceived impossibilities. I don't want any chumps in my life telling me, "You can't do that." I need champions who will challenge me to grow.

Relationships are magnets that either pull you closer to your destiny or they drive you away from it. Look at your relationships and ask yourself, "What kind of harvest have I received from the relationships that I have?" It is really important for you to evaluate your relationships because life without harvest is proof that you have invested in the wrong relationships.

**LQ Solution: Every relationship should be twofold:
you enhance the other person's life and that
person enhances yours.**

If you look at your relationships and see that everybody just takes and takes and takes from you with no harvest in return, it is proof that you have invested in the wrong soil. Stop investing in unproductive relationships and invest your time and energy into relationships that create a synergy between the two of you and both of you are growing. Review your relationships; disconnect from those relationships where there is no synergy. Everybody wants to go to the next level, but not everybody wants to disconnect from old relationships. They don't want to pay the price or experience the pain of letting go.

Your ability to lead effectively rests in your ability to pay the price of disconnecting from old relationships and embracing new relationships. Disconnecting is never pleasant and that is why most people never disconnect. They stay in a toxic environment; their lives never change. The Bible teaches us that evil influences good more than good influences evil. Scripture warns us to watch our relationships because corrupt people will corrupt us (see 1 Corinthians 15:33). You have to be willing to deal with the threshold of pain and disconnect from those relationships in order to go where you want to go.

LQ Solution: The reinvention triangle:
hire one, fire one, make one change.

As a coach, one of the first things I tell business leaders to do when they need fast change is: fire one person, hire one person that they need, and implement one change that they have been wanting to do—and do it now. It works every time.

You have to have the guts to fire one; and sometimes it is a family member, especially in the church. Some people aren't willing to go through the threshold of pain, so they keep people in positions who are not performing. One of your staff may be a spiritual son or daughter and it's difficult to release that person. Maybe one of the best things you can do for your child is to let him go so he can find the right relationship to grow and mature.

But if you won't make the change and handle the pain, your organization will stay the same. I will tell you from experience that everybody else in your organization has been praying for years for you to fire that person. When you do fire the person, you will become the hero. After you do it, you will wonder why you didn't let the person go ten years ago.

On the other hand, there is one person that you know you need with you to maximize who you are and what you are doing. But you can't hire that person because you are dragging along the anchor. You have to dare to make the change. I have worked with many companies, and I have never seen these three things fail to take the company to the next level. I believe it so much that I give a money-back guarantee. If your business doesn't explode after doing these three things, I will coach you for free until it does. I've never been called on it.

Proverbs 13:20 in *The Message* Bible says, "Become wise by walking with wise; hang out with fools and watch your life fall to pieces." In other words, hang out with unproductive people and your business will stagnate, your ministry will go nowhere. Get around wise people so that you will become wise yourself.

Ask yourself two questions:

1. *What investment have you made in yourself in the past year?* How much money have you spent on building what is between your two ears? Here is what I can tell you if you haven't invested in yourself—you are going nowhere. When you get on an airplane, one of the first things they tell you to do is put the oxygen mask on yourself first, then you can help somebody beside you. If you have not been putting any oxygen into yourself, you can't help anyone else. There is no empowerment going on.

2. *What have you been investing in other people?* What have you been giving to others? You need to take what you have learned and teach it to somebody else because when you teach something, it gets down inside you. You need to take what you have learned and teach it to

your children, your family. Turn off the television and tell your children about people. Tell them about God's love and how important it is to have a good attitude. Tell them the stories of Daniel and Joseph and Jonah. Let them know that there is good and evil in the world so they won't get discouraged about life.

A new commandment I give to you, that you love one another; as I have loved you, that you also love one another. By this all will know that you are My disciples, if you have love for one another (John 13:34-35 NKJV).

People will connect with you as a leader because you will give them what they cannot get anywhere else: love, acceptance, and forgiveness.

Here are some important truths I have learned about relationships:

- You cannot lead people if you don't love them.

- You will learn from people you like. You will follow people you love.

- Relationships shape your destiny!

- There is no such thing as a nonconsequential relationship.

- Abraham tried to take two wrong people into his future: Torah and Lot.

- You can fail all by yourself. You need a team of people to help you succeed. You must put people strategically in your life so you will not fail.

- If you do not live with accountability, you will die with regrets. Do not go into your tomorrow regretting what you did in your yesterday.

- All believers need a Paul over them, a Timothy under them, and a Barnabas beside them.

LQ Solution: Get the right people on the bus and get them into the right positions.

Every relationship you have is either blessing you or killing you. In a small church that has ten people on the leadership team, if three or four people on the team are out of place, you have a 33 percent dysfunction. In a megasize church with one hundred leaders and only three or four are out of place, you have only 3 percent dysfunction. The smaller the ministry, the more important it is that people be properly placed.

Jim Collins writes in his book, *Good to Great,* "We think to move good leaders to great would begin by getting a new vision and strategy. We have found instead that they first got the right people on the bus, the wrong people off the bus, and the right people in the right seats, and then they figured out where to drive it. The old adage 'People are your most important asset' turns out to be wrong. People are not your greatest asset, the right people are."

Unleash Your LQ

List the five top people in your life that you call a friend in a covenant relationship with you:

1. _____

2. _____

3. _____

4. _____

5. _____

List five people, who are above you, with whom you want to start developing a relationship:

1. _____

2. _____

3. _____

4. _____

5. _____

List five peers with whom you want to develop better friendships:

1. _____

2. _____

3. _____

4. _____

5. _____

List five people, below you, with whom you want to start investing your life:

1. _____

2. _____

3. _____

4. _____

5. _____

Be a Sailboat

You're a sailboat—not a rowboat. Raise the sails of spiritual disciplines to catch the wind of God's Spirit. It takes a team working together to raise the sails on a mighty war galleon—the Church. Equip your team to worship, work, witness, and stay in the Word so that you can catch the Spirit's wind and go where He goes.

–Dr. Larry Keefauver
The Presence-Driven Church

CHAPTER FOURTEEN

THE SHIP
YOU MUST
NOW SAIL

We have explored the acronym L.E.A.D.E.R. What about the S.H.I.P. that completes the word *leadership?*

There are many "ships" that move you through life: friendships, companionships, memberships, stewardships, and championships. However, there is only one "ship" that will help you reach your destiny and full potential—*God-empowered leadership.*

Let's break down the word leadership like a professional football coach would break down a play.

- **LEAD**: To show the way, to have a vision, to be in charge, to be responsible for results.

- **ER:** The letters "er" are in the middle of the word. Their position reflects balance and the intangible qualities that are not in the job description.

- **SHIP:** A ship is a vessel that is used to move cargo or people or an idea. A course must be charted or the ship and the crew will wander aimlessly. If you don't make constant adjustments for the wind, weather, seas, and the destination, you will be lost.

Leadership can be defined as the act of taking charge and handling the delicate balancing act of pushing, pulling, and working alongside others as you navigate your crew and their cargo to a common goal or destination.

If your vision is small and self-centered, all you really need for the journey is a one-person canoe. If you are going to achieve something great that will help all of humanity, you will need to travel in a great ship, like a war galleon, not a canoe or rowboat. Every ship requires a team of people to help you reach your desired destination.

LQ Solution: The greatest decision a leader has to make is who they allow on their team.

Jesus spent forty days fasting and praying before He picked His twelve-member team. He still picked one who was a thief and a betrayer. Always remember, any person in your life has the potential of becoming a Judas in your life. A person in the church was stealing offerings. The first question the investigators asked the pastor to do was to list the top ten people in his organization that he trusted the most. Why? Statistics reveal that when theft is taking place, it usually involves the most trusted people. Not everyone who starts with you will stay with you for the long haul.

The story of Jonah teaches us that all you need is one wrong person on your SHIP, and they can cause the entire ship to be caught up in a storm. The other men on the ship were innocent bystanders of the negative effects of having Jonah on the boat with them. What do you do when you discover you have a Jonah on the boat with you? Simple—kick Jonah off the boat! As soon as Jonah was off the boat, the storm calmed. There will be storms of negativity—the strength of the ship and the team is tested only in the storm.

SHIP

Increasing your LQ begins with improving your mindset and bringing your inner life to its highest level. Successful leaders today will stand firm in the storms versus being knocked down by all the economic and cultural storms around them. Those who improve their LQ will invest in bulletproofing their mind-set while staying strong on the inside. A staggeringly successful outer life starts by having a staggeringly successful inner life. Focus and confidence matter! The inner life of a leader and the leadership team around him or her determines the success of the journey. The people around you need to reflect the qualities you exemplify which are:

S —Security
H —Humility
I —Insightful
P —Passion

S – Security

Security provides the foundation for strong leadership. When leaders feel insecure, they drift from their purpose whenever trouble arises. Leaders must feel secure when people stop liking them, when funding or profit drops, when morale dips, or when others reject them. If a leader does not feel secure, fear will eventually cause them to sabotage their leadership influence. I have a lot of coaching material to help you as a leader increase your confidence levels. Security is rooted in confidence, which leads to success.

So what is confidence?

Confidence is a positive belief in yourself, your potential, and your abilities. Confidence produces a feeling of certainty, and hope empowering you to perform at your best, create workable solutions to your problems, think big about your future, take calculated risks, and act effectively to achieve extraordinary, outrageous results—and success for you and others.

Confidence is the bridge between where you are and where you want to go.

H – Humility

Notice that I never refer to confidence as pride. Confidence in leaders springs from an inner humility that seeks to serve rather than be served. Humility continually asks, "What's in this for your best?" instead of inquiring, "What's in this for me?" Humility is not thinking less of yourself; it is thinking less about yourself because you are focused on the successes or achievements of others.

It is against the law for a captain to abandon ship. Why? Because it violates the number one law of leadership: think of others first, not about yourself. Servant leadership arises from the attitude that Paul writes about in Philippians 2:1-11 (NKJV).

Humility declares that my confidence is in the Lord (see Proverbs 3:26). The humble leader can be confident without being proud, assertive without being aggressive or passive, enthusiastic without being hyped, and encouraging without ulterior motives.

I – Insightful Intelligence

The person with insight has an inner perspective that discerns using godly wisdom from the Word of God. God's perspective takes the long look with an eternal perspective. Insightful intelligence uses the mind of Christ that surpasses common sense, human education and degrees, and life experience. Yes, education, experience, and practical understanding all have their contribution to make to leadership, but insightful intelligence rooted in godly wisdom with the mind of Christ gives the leader a biblical mind-set within which to make right decisions instead of just good ones.

Insightful intelligence takes biblical wisdom, knowledge, and understanding to the highest level of application in daily life. Are you willing to keep Christ continually in sight (*insightful*), to fix your eyes on Him (see Hebrews 12:2) so that the mind of Christ (intelligence) becomes the lens through which you view every person and situation?

P – Passion

I have studied the lives of great men and famous women, and I found that the men and women who got to the top were those who did the jobs they had in hand, with everything they had of energy and enthusiasm. –Harry S. Truman

There is no greatness without a passion to be great, whether it's the aspiration of an athlete, an artist, scientist, parent, or businessperson. It's passion that drives people to stay up late and get up early. Many people are passionate, but because of their limiting beliefs about who they are and what they can do, they never take the actions that could make their dream a reality. Your passion has to be greater than your obstacle, or your obstacle will eat you for breakfast.

The change agent's message will always be attacked. Passion speaks of suffering as well. Passion means to suffer—think *The Passion of Christ.* Leaders suffer. They go through tough stuff. Leaders are willing walk through tests, trials, and tribulation, knowing they are all parts of the process of growing and maturing. Paul writes about godly passion and suffering as well, *"And not only that, but we also glory in tribulations, knowing that tribulation produces perseverance; and perseverance, character; and character, hope. Now hope does not disappoint, because the love of God has been poured out in our hearts by the Holy Spirit who was given to us"* (Romans 5:3-5 NKJV). Be passionate. Stay in the process. Be willing to endure the glory of tribulation!

Your SHIP may be beaten up and battered by the war but you are still sailing toward your desired destination. You are called as a leader to be a godly example, to change lives, create wealth, and transform culture. Real cultural transformation happens when leaders determine in their hearts that they are not going to allow the culture to define them, detour them, or set them off course. This is your destiny.

True leadership development is never a quick fix! You have boarded the SHIP of leadership. Set sail with your eyes looking forward, with the wind of the Spirit on your back, the compass of God's Word in your hand, and the weapon of a highly developed and trained leadership army on deck for greater influence, impact, and income as you lead others to their destinies in Christ!

THE LQ
SOLUTION
PROFILE

This assessment allows you to measure where you see yourself with regard to your current level of leadership skills. Circle where you are right now in living out each statement, with 10 being the highest mark of assessment for each statement.

- 0 - Totally False

- 1-3 - Not Very Often

- 4-6 - Sometimes True Sometimes False

- 7-8 - Frequently True

- 9 - Mostly True

- 10 - Always True

L - Lead by Positive Example

I am constantly aware that somebody is watching my actions, attitudes, and appearance; so I confidently maintain a high standard of integrity and always choose words and actions that reflect godly values in all public and private settings.

0   1   2   3   4   5   6   7   8   9   10

E - Empowerment

I have developed my people skills so that I can provide my team with effective coaching and equipping by consistently treating people with dignity, by building confidence, by trusting people enough to release them into their calling and purpose, and by ensuring that people receive effective training for them to succeed and in turn empower others.

0   1   2   3   4   5   6   7   8   9   10

A - Attitude

I model a positive attitude and communicate a "can do" sense of urgency in getting the job done, especially in times of crisis, when problems or challenges arise, and when changes need to be implemented.

0   1   2   3   4   5   6   7   8   9   10

D - Destiny

I have a crystal clear picture of the future; I know and can write in one sentence my purpose in life; and I have a detailed written personal and organizational plan for the next five years envisioning how to maximize my influence, impact, and income in such a way that all those around me prosper and mature in their calling and destiny.

0   1   2   3   4   5   6   7   8   9   10

E - Excellence

My standard is to be world class at everything I do, so I am constantly thinking how I can improve what I am doing so I can be the best at what I do; my standards reflect God's best for myself and others so that others can imitate me and be like Christ.

0   1   2   3   4   5   6   7   8   9   10

R - Relationships

I am a team builder who values relationships more than money; I invest my time developing intimacy and transparency with my family, friends, coworkers, and new acquaintances in order to have a network of people who love God, others, and themselves sincerely.

0   1   2   3   4   5   6   7   8   9   10

S - Security

As a big thinker, I have a very positive belief in myself, my potential, and my future that gives me a feeling of certainty and confidence that I will succeed in whatever I attempt to do no matter what obstacles are standing in my way; as such, I possess a tenacious persistence that refuses to allow obstacles or failure to distract me from finishing what God has called me to accomplish.

0   1   2   3   4   5   6   7   8   9   10

H - Humility

I know my worth, so I think less about myself and more about adding value, solving problems, and meeting the needs of others; I understand that my identity in Christ qualifies and positions me to be a servant leader and in humility reproduce leaders who are salt and light change agents who transform lives and culture.

0   1   2   3   4   5   6   7   8   9   10

I - Insight

I make my decisions based on eternity and proven biblical principles; I intentionally seek to acquire the technological knowledge and skills needed to succeed in tomorrow's world; my insight uses wisdom, knowledge, and understanding to help myself and others clarify who we are and who were are becoming as godly leaders.

0   1   2   3   4   5   6   7   8   9   10

P - Passion

I am an inspirational leader who is motivated by my huge dream and a purpose that ignites excitement and energy enabling me to effectively steward time, money, and people's work so that I don't burn out but rather impassion others with zeal to accomplish good works that glorify God.

0   1   2   3   4   5   6   7   8   9   10

_____ Total Score

Your LQ score is: _____

- A total score less than 70 represents *significant underdeveloped potential as a leader.*

- A total score between 70-80 represents *emerging understanding of your potential as a leader.*

- A total score between 81-90 represents *developing actualization of your leadership abilities.*

- A total score over 90 represents *a maturing wisdom, knowledge, and understanding of what God requires of you as a leader.*

What three sections did you score the highest?

1. _____

2. _____

3. _____

What are three areas you need to develop?

1. _____

2. _____

3. _____

What plan are you going to implement in your life to change these problem areas?

_____

_____

_____

_____

_____

_____

THE LQ COACHING SYSTEM

Join the LQ Movement!

Smart leaders invest time, money, and effort in adding value to their team.
—Dr. Keith Johnson

Package includes:

- 5 Paperback Copies of *The LQ Solution* Book
- 4 Live CD and 4 Live DVD Teachings of LQ
- 1 PDF Digital Copy of the Teacher's Manuel
- 1 PDF Digital Copy of the Student Manuel
- 1 PDF Digital Copy of LQ Test
- 1 PDF Digital Copy of LQ Profile Short
- 1 PDF Digital Copy of LQ Intensive Profile Long
- 1 PDF Digital Copy of 360° LQ Profile

5 Paperback Copies of THE LQ SOLUTION

Live LQ Teaching
4 CDs/4 DVDs

 PDF Digital Copies of:

For More Information Visit:
www.LQSolution.com

LEADERSHIP COACHING

Choose to be Coached by America's #1 Confidence Coach

Many successful leaders spend a lot of time coaching and consulting others within their organizations, but many times being "top dog" can be a lonely place. The million-dollar questions: Who coaches the coach? Who coaches the Senior Pastor or CEO? Who coaches the business owner? Who coaches the leaders of any organization?

Every great athlete needs a coach—and so do you!

As a leader, ask yourself: Do I have someone in my life who is not impressed with my current accomplishments or status who will stretch me toward my maximum potential?

Smart leaders leverage the advantages of a personal consultant or coach.

Most life, leadership, and business coaches omit the very important aspect of spirituality and making decisions according to God's Word. Dr. Keith Johnson, America's #1 Confidence Coach, is the person you can seek counsel from to receive biblically-based solutions, experienced spiritual advice, and proven leadership coaching answers.

For more information about Dr. Johnson's Leadership Coaching Programs, contact:

Online:
www.KeithJohnson.TV/coaching

Telephone:
352-597-8775

Email:
Info@KeithJohnson.TV

DESTINY COLLEGE

RESOURCES

More Books by Dr. Keith Johnson

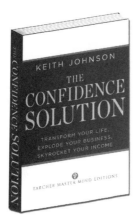
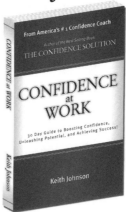

The Confidence Solution
Confidence at Work

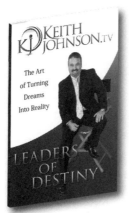

Leaders of Destiny
Leading in Crisis Times

Visit KeithJohnson.TV to Order!

Confidence Coaching System

Maximize your confidence in only 30 days with the Confidence Coaching System so you can:

- Experience outrageous success in life.

- Increase your happiness.

- Double your income.

- Fall in love with yourself.

- Quickly change bad habits.

- Speed up your destiny.

- Create the amazing success you deserve!

The Confidence Coaching System empowers you to become a confident and successful person by recognizing your inner strengths and talents. Dr. Keith Johnson coaches you through a 30-day journey designed to reveal your potential and boost your best qualities. Drawing on the secrets of successful people, he shares easy-to-understand strategies that will maximize performance in every area of your life.

Order Online: *www.KeithJohnson.TV*

Stop Dreaming and Start Writing!

Dr. Keith Johnson's Writers' Boot Camp

There is a best-selling book hidden inside of YOU!

Do you dream of writing a book? Dr. Keith Johnson will show you how to take your dream of writing a best-selling book and make it a reality. Here are just a few secrets Dr. Keith reveals in this informative boot camp experience:

- How to take your book from an idea, to paper, to print.

- How you can become a multimillionaire selling information.

- Seven reasons why you need to write a book.

- How to use your book to get radio and television interviews.

- The "ins" and "outs" of obtaining an agent and publisher.

- How to get a publisher to accept your book.

- How to market your book to become a bestseller.

- And much more.

Book Writers' package includes:

- Teacher's Manual

- Student Manual

- 7 CDs recorded live at the conference

Order Online: *www.KeithJohnson.TV*

The Confidence Solution Intensive

DR. KEITH JOHNSON

Keith Johnson is known as one of the premier speakers on the subjects of Christian leadership, confidence building, and strategic planning. For the past sixteen years, his messages, books, and leadership coaching has helped some of the largest and most prestigious churches in the world to experience spiritual, numerical, and financial growth.

Keith's journey to becoming recognized by other leaders as America's #1 Confidence Coach did not start out well. He failed kindergarten; and by the time he was in fifth grade, he could barely read and write and almost failed again.

His parents divorced, and his father became an alcoholic, drug addict, and joined a motorcycle club called Satan's Escorts. His own father introduced him to drugs at the young age of thirteen; and by sixteen, his father taught him how to sell drugs for a living. His mother married an alcoholic who was very abusive to the entire family.

Keith experienced a radical encounter with Jesus Christ when he was twenty-two years of age. He was instantly set free from alcoholism, drugs, and a promiscuous lifestyle.

Keith's biblically-based success and leadership principles have now influenced both the church and secular markets. His recent book, *The Confidence Solution—Reinvent Yourself, Explode Your Business, Skyrocket Your Income* became a bestseller by reaching

#21 in Amazon's motivation and business category. He is a frequent television guest, appearing on popular shows and stations such as New York's PIX 11, *Fox Business News*, *The Tom Sullivan Show*, CBS, ABC, and many others. He has been recognized by *Women's World* magazine as one of America's "Ultimate Experts," which is the most-read women's magazine in the world.

Keith Johnson, PhD, is a dedicated lifelong learner. He earned a Master's of Christian Leadership and a Doctor of Philosophy in Theology from Christian Life University. He is the founder of Destiny College International, an accredited college specializing in graduate training for pastors and business leaders. He is a certified speaker, trainer, and coach for the John Maxwell team.

Invite Dr. Keith Johnson to speak at your next event!

www.KeithJohnson.TV/Speaking

Toll Free: 888-379-2663